INSTANT PROMOTIONS

Action International
Business Coaching

Other Books in the Instant Success Series

Successful Franchising by Bradley J. Sugars
The Real Estate Coach by Bradley J. Sugars
Billionaire in Training by Bradley J. Sugars
Instant Cashflow by Bradley J. Sugars
Instant Sales by Bradley J. Sugars
Instant Leads by Bradley J. Sugars
Instant Profit by Bradley J. Sugars
Instant Repeat Business by Bradley J. Sugars
Instant Team Building by Bradley J. Sugars
Instant Systems by Bradley J. Sugars
Instant Referrals by Bradley J. Sugars
Instant Advertising by Bradley J. Sugars
The Business Coach by Bradley J. Sugars

INSTANT PROMOTIONS

BRADLEY J. SUGARS

McGraw-Hill

New York   Chicago   San Francisco   Lisbon   London
Madrid   Mexico City   Milan   New Delhi   San Juan
Seoul   Singapore   Sydney   Toronto

1 2 3 4 5 6 7 8 9 0   FGR/FGR   0 9 8 7 6 5

ISBN 0-07-146665-7

This publication is designed to provide accurate and authoritative information in regard to the subject matter covered. It is sold with the understanding that neither the author nor the publisher is engaged in rendering legal, accounting, or other professional service. If legal advice or other expert assistance is required, the services of a competent professional person should be sought.
—From a Declaration of Principles jointly adopted by Committee of the American Bar Association and a Committee of Publishers.

McGraw-Hill books are available at special quantity discounts to use as premiums and sales promotions, or for use in corporate training programs. For more information, please write to the Director of Special Sales, McGraw-Hill Professional, Two Penn Plaza, New York, NY 10121-2298. Or contact your local bookstore.

Sugars, Bradley J.
  Instant promotions / Bradley J. Sugars.
    p. cm.
  ISBN 0-07-146665-7 (alk. paper)
1. Advertising campaigns. I. Title.
  HF5837.S84 2006
659.1'13—dc22   2005025417

To all *Action* Business Coaches,
leaders in every sense of the word.

▮ Contents

▌ Introduction

Have you heard the saying; "Build a better mousetrap, and the market will beat a path to your door?"

It's rubbish.

Many years ago, when we were still well and truly in the industrial age, manufacturers thought all they had to do was to produce a great product and it would sell itself. They thought people would stampede to get their hands on it.

That was before they understood anything about marketing. You see, they had yet to discover the secret that true business success occurs in understanding the needs and desires of the market. Of consumers. Or to put it more plainly, of people.

Business leaders and thinkers then worked out that if they were to identify what it was people needed, then concentrated on producing just that, they would have a ready market.

But even doing this didn't guarantee them overnight success. It wouldn't necessarily result in consumers' falling over each other to get to the store to buy.

Why? Because if they, the consumers, didn't know the product was available, and if they didn't know where to go to get it, how could they clamor for it, even if they had the money?

Of course, we know they couldn't. And so did the smart businesspeople at the time.

They knew they had to *promote* the product and their business.

This is still the position we are in today. How can you expect people to buy from you if they don't know about you or what you sell? It's quite simple, isn't it? In fact, I'd say it's rather obvious. Yet how many businesses in this advanced technological age—this age of information—actually devote any of their resources to *promotion*?

Sure, they might place a small ad in the local paper, or they might do a mailbox drop of the local area from time to time. And they might have a flashy visible presence, a good-looking shop with a nicely sign-written window, but is that enough?

Understand this: The key to successful promotion is consistency. You need to develop promotion strategies that promote your business in a consistent, deliberate manner and on a regular basis. That could be every day, every week, every month, or in some situations, all the time. It's a planned activity. It's not something that just happens.

The greatest businesspeople and marketers are not necessarily the smartest or the most innovative. Most simply understand the concept of testing and measuring.

When you are testing and measuring, there is no failure (except the failure to record your results and analyze them). Every step brings you closer to the right formula, and the right approach. If you approach your marketing expecting everything to work the first time, you'll be bitter and disappointed when you discover it doesn't. You may give up before you should.

Remember this: Marketing has certain rules, but it's still largely a matter of trial and error. You give it your best guess, and then find out for sure. It's essential that you meticulously record every result. It's extra work, but you'll be glad when you have a marketing strategy you know will produce results. That confidence comes only from testing and measuring.

There's one more concept I'd like to introduce before we go much further. That is the concept of the *relationship*. It's important that you understand what relationships can do for your business. You see, one of the powerful results promotional campaigns bring to any business is the relationship that develops between the business and its target market. If you enjoy a good relationship with your customers, they will trust what you say to them. They will be more likely to take the advice or recommendation of your salespeople than if the relationship was nonexistent or poor.

There's another very important aspect of the concept of relationship. If you have a good relationship with your target markets, you'll find it very much easier to run promotional campaigns. You'll find your promotional campaigns will become reiterative. They will be easier to repeat. This, in turn, will result in still better relationships with your target markets, in better brand recognition, and in better acceptance in the marketplace.

A little dubious, you think? Not at all. Just look at the big players. Take Coca-Cola, for instance. Do you think this company really needs to invest the millions it does on promotional activities even though the product probably enjoys one of the highest levels of brand recognition anywhere in the world? Of course it does. If Coca-Cola were to back off just a little, the company would lose vital ground to its opposition. It's all about top-of-mind awareness. And because Coca-Cola is a well-recognized company, it enjoys a very good relationship with various target markets. This makes it far easier for it to generate good publicity. Coca-Cola's press releases aren't tossed aside by journalists quite as quickly as those from other lesser-known companies.

Companies like Coca-Cola have been doing this for a very long time, too. And the company does it in a systematic way. Its promotional machine has developed momentum, but the company needs to keep it rolling. If it were to slacken off, it would lose momentum. Of that you can be certain.

So what then does the term *promotion* actually mean? What areas of business are covered by it?

According to the dictionary, the word "promote" means to "help the progress of." Isn't that interesting?

With this in mind, what business activities does this cover? Well, a whole lot actually. But before I mention them, I'm going to remind you first of another very important concept. This is the concept I call the Business Chassis. (Read more about this in my book *Instant Cashflow*.)

Refer to the Business Chassis diagram on the next page.

Promotion works on the first part of the Business Chassis—the leads. Promotional activities are those designed to bring in leads. They involve activities like PR and advertising, and I'm sure most of you will be familiar with these, at least in general terms. But there are other, less obvious, activities that are just as important when it comes to promoting your business. Things like sponsorships, in-store signage, window displays, network functions, and seminars, to mention but a few.

You'll learn all you need to know about these different promotional activities through reading this book.

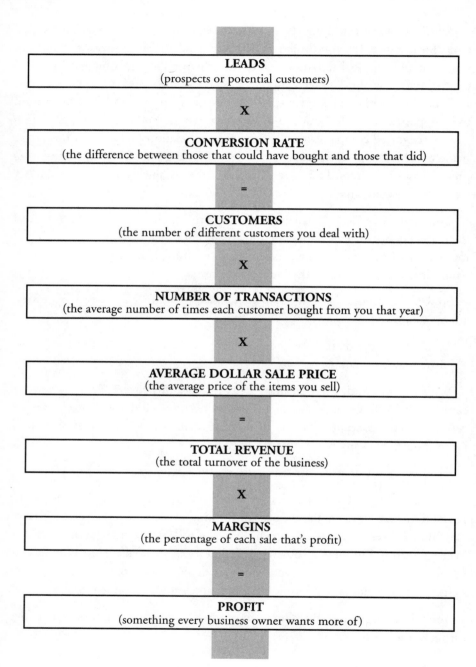

LEADS
(prospects or potential customers)

X

CONVERSION RATE
(the difference between those that could have bought and those that did)

=

CUSTOMERS
(the number of different customers you deal with)

X

NUMBER OF TRANSACTIONS
(the average number of times each customer bought from you that year)

X

AVERAGE DOLLAR SALE PRICE
(the average price of the items you sell)

=

TOTAL REVENUE
(the total turnover of the business)

X

MARGINS
(the percentage of each sale that's profit)

=

PROFIT
(something every business owner wants more of)

So, congratulations on deciding to take proactive steps to promote your business. By concentrating on first things first, you'll set in motion a chain of activities that will generate more leads for your business. I personally guarantee it.

This book is designed to give you the inside track on everything you need to know about promoting your business. It aims to provide you with an *instant* guide on how to produce the various promotional items just like the professionals. Once you've read the book, you'll know precisely what it takes to successfully promote your business.

This book is the next step in your marketing success story. From this moment on, you won't have to dream about the day when you're recognized as a leader in your field. You'll know precisely what to do to make it a reality. You'll also know exactly how to go about generating more leads for your business.

■ How to Use This Book

This book is divided into different parts, one for each of the major promotional tools I'll be discussing.

Pick the part that interests you most, jump right in, and begin working through the steps outlined. Each step covers an important aspect of the promotional tool being discussed. You see, there are things you must give careful consideration to before getting carried away doing the "fun" things involved in promoting your business.

Of course, there are certain elements that are common to all the promotional tools being discussed, so these will be handled in detail in Part 6 towards the end of the book. Read them in conjunction with the various parts of the book that deal with particular promotional tools.

You might decide to implement the great ideas explained in this book all at once. Or you might decide to implement them one at a time. But whatever you decide, the important thing is that you'll no longer be blundering around in the dark, unsure whether what you're doing has a chance of bringing in more business or not.

We'll begin by catching up with my mechanic, Charlie, who decided it was time he began promoting his business. Now those who know him will know that he's no business tycoon. He doesn't even have a business head. But he soon realized the need for promotion. Follow his experiences and learn as he did about the role promotion can play in any business. You'll discover, like he did, the power of promotion and how it can turn your business around.

You might also be surprised at how much this exercise will reveal about your business. It may get you thinking about important issues that have never crossed your mind before. If some of this information is new to you, don't be concerned—there's never been a better time to start promoting your business.

Make sure you make notes as you go along. When you come to designing your own promotional tools, you'll find it useful referring back to them. You'll find proven examples and ideas that, when combined with your new knowledge, will bring results.

Now it's time to get started—there are customers out there waiting to deal with you. All you need is the right form of promotion.

■ Charlie Learns the Power of Promotion

Over the years I had gotten to know Charlie, my mechanic, very well. He had always done an extremely good job on servicing my cars, and as far as I was concerned, his mechanical knowledge was first-rate.

Being a satisfied customer, I'd always been quick to refer my friends and acquaintances to him. And I've every reason to believe other satisfied customers would be doing the same.

I watched with more than a little interest as his business grew. He now employs four mechanics who are also beginning to gain something of a reputation for themselves.

However, over the last few months, Charlie has begun to talk frankly with me about matters other than cars. He started hinting that all was not quite as well as he'd like as far as his business was concerned. Then, one day when I was having new tires mounted on my car, he began asking me what he could do to improve the viability of his business. I responded by taking him to visit a few of my clients, the intention being that he could see for himself what others are doing as far as managing their businesses is concerned.

The end result was that he asked me to become his Coach. I agreed and began by exploring various options he had to increase his number of leads. Read about this in my book *Instant Leads*.

Charlie was delighted and couldn't wait until our next session, which would focus on promoting his business. And neither could I.

So it was with more than a little excitement that I pulled up outside his garage, parked the car, and headed for the office door.

"Good morning, Brad," he shouted. He had heard the rumble of my car's engine as it idled.

"Good morning, Charlie. How are things?"

"Good. Come on in. I can't wait to get started."

His small office had been prepared for my visit—the usually cluttered desk was clear, two chairs were waiting on the same side of the desk, and coffee was boiling.

"You're eager to get started this morning," I quipped as he showed me into the office. I could tell he wasn't going to talk cars first, and I wasn't sure whether I was glad or sad. I always looked forward to visiting Charlie precisely because he was a fountain of knowledge when it came to cars, and I really enjoyed our discussions. However, I was beginning to sense he now looked forward to my visits for a similar reason, although now the subject was business, not cars.

"Brad, I'm now really eager to step my business up a gear. What are we going to work on this time?"

"It's now time we think about promoting your business, Charlie. You need to put in place strategies aimed at letting as many people as possible know what you can do for them."

"Great. I've always liked the idea of promoting my garage. I think I'll be good at that too. What's it take?"

"It's a little more involved than that. But don't worry, I'm going to help you right from the beginning. You see, there's nothing mystical about promoting a business. It's pretty straightforward and logical, once you know how. But first, can I ask you what your competitors are doing that you feel is effective?"

"Let me think—Johnny's Servo produces a newsletter that he drops in the glove box of every car he services, and that seems to work quite well. Customers of mine have mentioned it to me. Then there's the Tire and Mechanical guy down the road who always seems to be distributing brochures. They look good and customers like them for the special offers he advertises."

"That's great, Charlie. Now, do your competitors affect you directly, or is there enough business out there for you all?"

"I guess there's never enough business, Brad. You know, I'd sure like to have a bigger slice of the pie, but how would I cope? Then on the other hand, I never know from one week to the next how busy I'm going to be. If I could just get a better handle on that, I'd be making huge progress. But the bottom line is, sure, my competitors do affect my business. I know when they're running special deals, and I don't get their advertising material—my workshop is my barometer!"

"OK, Charlie, what I want you to do now is tell me what three things come to mind when I mention the word 'clients.' What springs to mind?"

"Money, work, and being able to meet my obligations. Is that what you mean?"

"Yeah, that's just fine. Now, some of the clients I've worked with have been limited by the type of marketing they can do. For example, optometrists can't by law advertise to their past customers to get them to come back for an eye test for a period of two years. Is there anything that you can't do in relation to advertising and marketing?"

"No, nothing like that, Brad. The only thing limiting me is my lack of business knowledge."

Even though this line of questioning would probably be thought of as boring and mundane to Charlie, I could tell he was not losing interest. But I could tell he was beginning to wonder where all this was going.

"OK, Charlie, I'm nearly done—with this process anyway. Last question— do you have any unconverted prospects?"

"What do you mean, Brad?"

"Sorry, I should have explained. Unconverted prospects are people who made contact with you, for a quote or an idea of what might be wrong with their cars for instance, yet never came back to have the job done. They're the people who you never did end up doing business with."

"Oh yes, I have plenty of those! But don't ask me how many or who they are. I wouldn't have a clue."

"Well, this is your next major lesson in marketing, Charlie. *Always* keep contact details of all your prospects. You see, by doing so you'll be building up a fantastic, and priceless, database of people who are interested in what you can do for them. It's a resource many businesses pay good money to get ahold of. And it's something you can base your entire marketing effort on."

"How do I do that, Brad?"

"There are no hard-and-fast rules. You can do it any way you feel comfortable with. Start by drawing up a simple form that has headings such as name, address, telephone number, make of car, registration number, nature of initial inquiry, date, outcome, and date of initial and repeat purchases. This can be entered into your computer or it can be stored alphabetically in a file—whatever suits you best. But whatever you do, start collecting details *right now*."

Charlie was beginning to enjoy himself. I could tell he wasn't feeling as insecure now as when I when I first arrived. He could follow the logic of what we were discussing.

"I never knew business could actually be fun, Brad. I'm beginning to enjoy myself already."

"That's the whole point—it *must* be fun. Why else would you get involved? Far better to just get a job if you weren't going to have fun running your own business. So let's get right in and have some fun. What do you say, Charlie?"

"Now you're talking. I sense that you've got something up your sleeve, Brad."

"I do. I'm now going to show you, step-by-step, how to actually go about putting together various publications that will bring you in more business. And on top of that, they're fun to do."

"Sounds great, Brad. What are they?"

"I'm talking about press releases, direct mail, brochures, flyers, and office stationery. But don't be alarmed—they're easy to do, and you'll have a great deal of fun putting them together. And no, they're not the sort of things only professional graphic design gurus can do! You can and should do it yourself, and I'm now going to show you how."

INSTANT PROMOTIONS

$$\boxed{\textbf{Part 1}}$$

■ Press Releases

Charlie, the first thing we'll look at today is a marketing tool called a press release. Some call it a media release or a news release. It's the same thing. Got that?"

"Yeah, man. No worries. But isn't that something those fancy PR-types need to do?"

"Not really, Charlie. Once you know how, it's very easy. Not only that, they can be a really effective way of getting expensive publicity for your business, for free."

"Yes, I realize how powerful they can be. That's why I always assumed they need to be produced by expensive PR firms. And I never really had the money to pay for that."

"There are lots of businesses that have the same idea, Charlie. And that's why when you begin producing your own, you'll gain an important advantage over your opposition. So, let's get started, shall we?"

What Is a Successful Press Release?

Simply speaking, any press release that first gets published, and second leads to increased store traffic and sales, is successful. But press releases aren't just used to increase business. They play a very important role in helping to change perceptions or counter negative publicity a business may have suffered.

Used properly, press releases are incredibly powerful promotional tools, and every business should make use of them.

Your aim, when writing a press release, is to get free publicity. Whether you're moving to a new location or launching a new product, if you can generate free media coverage, it's well worth it.

You need to understand the value of free publicity. Unlike advertising, where you are paying to reach a skeptical public, the beauty of press releases is they rely on independent people to promote your business for you. That's right—they result in journalists giving you coverage in their media.

The people rely on these journalists to give them the facts. And because they are independent, they are seen credible as sources of information. If a journalist says your product is the best on the market, the public will believe it.

What Makes a Successful Press Release?

There are a number of key elements that combine to make a successful press release. The most important of these is its appeal or news angle. I'll be discussing this a little later on.

The headline needs to convey the message quickly. I'll show you how to write effective headlines shortly. I'll also show you which photographs to include for maximum impact and what angles earn the highest readership. You'll also discover which section of the publication your story should appear in, as well as the correct length and layout for your press release.

The Seven Steps to Writing Successful Press Releases

Step 1: Who Are You Targeting?

You need to consider whom it is you want to read the story or article when it is eventually published, and whom it is you want to read the press release.

Let's consider the first one. We are talking here about those who make up your target market. They are the people who do business with you now, as well as those you'd like to do business with in the future.

Understand this: If you don't know who the members of your target market are, it's almost impossible to attract them to your business. Imagine trying to get a date without knowing the gender you're interested in? You'd be taking a "let's see" approach. Unfortunately, the "let's see" approach tends to fail every time when it comes to generating publicity for your business. You won't see any results in the media, and you certainly won't see any new customers.

You really do need to know exactly who you are dealing with, what their interests are, and what's going to make them buy from you. If you don't, you're really just taking your chances.

So let's get specific. What people are most likely to be interested in your product or service? Here are some guidelines:

Age: How old are they? Don't just say all ages. I want to create a picture in your mind of your average customers. Think of an age that represents most of them.

Sex: Are they male or female? Half and half is too broad. Practically every business is split one way or the other. Give it some real thought. Who spends more and visits most often?

Income: How much do they earn? Do they make a great living (in which case quality would be an issue), or are they scraping for every dollar and always looking for the best deal? It's essential that you find this out.

Where do they live? Are they local, or do they come from miles around to deal with you? This will be important when deciding how to communicate with them.

What are their interests? This is important to know when writing a press release. If you don't know what interests them, how are you going to know what sort of article will interest them?

Now let's consider the other important target of your press release—the person who will be reading it. No, I don't mean the readers who make up your target market. I mean the person who'll read it way before the target market ever does. This is the journalist you want to make contact with to get your press release published. This is closely linked with Step 2, so consider this journalist part and parcel of the same topic.

To work out whom to address your press release to, call the publication or station that you want to target, and ask who looks after the relevant section or program. You'll find out more about how to go about contacting these people later on, but for now, you simply need to know who the journalist is.

Step 2: Where Should You Run Your Article?

Now that you've identified whom you want to target, you need to find a publication or station that reaches them. There may be a number of suitable options, so to find out which could work best for you, try them all, and test and measure the results.

Of course, there's no reason why you can't send your press release to anyone you think might run with it. Understand that you're not paying for this exposure. Regardless of how many people read the publication or listen to the station, it can still be very worthwhile. The only time you'll have to restrict whom you send your press release to is when you're offering a scoop, but more on that later.

Think about what radio stations that members of your target market listen to, what television stations they watch, and what they read. Then consider what sections of those publications or stations they prefer.

Newspapers are the most common recipients of press releases. Newspaper publicity can be quite effective, as people tend to hold onto the paper, and you can include more detail than you can with radio and television.

Here's a brief outline of the major types of publications best suited for press releases:

Daily Newspapers

These are papers that are published six or seven days a week. Circulation figures can vary greatly from day to day. They have larger circulations than weekly papers and attract wealthier readers. If you sell expensive items, luxury services, or have a sale that lasts only a few days, then daily publications are more effective than weeklies.

Weekly Newspapers

These are published once a week and are usually delivered free of charge to homes. Because they are delivered to specific areas, they can be very effective for businesses that target low-income earners.

Magazines

Because most magazines are national publications, they will generally not be interested in local news stories. You need to make sure your story has wide appeal to stand a chance here. Magazines offer one major advantage—they target people with specific interests. For example, a company that manufactures bull bars would send its press release to a 4WD magazine, and a hose manufacturer could target a gardening magazine.

Trade Journals

These tend to have very low readership levels. They often rely on companies' sending in press releases, and in this way source information for articles. It's normally very easy to get coverage in these publications.

Newsletters

Schools, sporting groups, and other organizations may have newsletters that you can run articles in. Because of their low circulation and limited content, most will not be worth your time and effort. However, they can provide useful publicity, especially if you live in a small community or regional area or if the newsletter is popular with a specific industry.

Local Radio

You may be able to request when your story runs, as most radio stations have local news updates on a regular basis. Of course, if your story is big enough, there's no reason why it wouldn't get a mention during every update. Remember this: You're not paying for this publicity. How, where, and when your press release is used is purely at the discretion of the journalists involved.

Local Television

When dealing with your local TV station, you're probably going to be limited as to when your story will be run. Most stations have only one or two hours allocated to local stories each evening.

Step 3: What Are You Going to Say?

There are probably many things you'd like to say to promote your business. But you need to remember the media are not there as your free advertising vehicle. If what you have to say isn't newsworthy, it won't be used.

To give you an idea of what I mean, let's look at a store that imports rugs. If the store is having a sale, it would probably like to say something like, "Huge sale, 70 percent off all rugs." The problem with this is it sounds like an ad. It doesn't have a news angle.

Now if they were to approach it from a different angle, it could get exceptional coverage. The store could say, "The decline of overseas currencies is killing small business." It could go on to say that because of the decline of the Asian dollar, cheap rugs are flooding the market. It could say it has had to reduce its top-quality stock by up to 70 percent, and if the current trend continues, many other local businesses could soon be feeling the pinch.

Notice how a different angle can change a story. You can still get your basic message across—that you are having a sale—only this time you give the impression that your stock is better and that buyers need to beware of cheaper, inferior products.

If a press release doesn't have a news angle, it won't get published. Don't even waste your time trying. You need to be saying something to your potential readers; there must be a strong story line to attract their interest. Any selling message you include must be subtle. It mustn't get in the way of the story. Remember, this kind of unpaid promotion is a great way to get your name out there in the marketplace. Try to find an important point of difference or unusual benefit for customers to deal with you, as well as a newsworthy angle.

Keep in mind that "news" must be just that. Writing a press release about a product that's been on the market for years just won't work. It needs to contain something new and interesting.

Let's consider what a newsworthy point of difference might be. Stop and think for a moment about the things that make your business unusual. Then ask yourself whether those differences are truly newsworthy. For example, if you want to promote a steak and seafood restaurant, you'd be hard pressed to stand out. But what if your steakhouse offered to drive patrons home, in their own cars, after they'd had too much to drink? That would certainly be worth promoting.

Try and find a human-interest angle. For example, if a real estate agent had sold 42 houses to a particular family over a 78-year period that covered three generations, the family could speak about the exceptional customer service that kept it coming back.

Perhaps you can find a newsworthy angle. Perhaps you've just opened a new room in your restaurant where customers get a massage before they dine. Perhaps you have an author coming to your restaurant for a book-signing session. You might have been given a prestigious award, or had one of your staff do something amazing for a customer. If something has happened that has genuine interest value, let people know about it. But remember, it must be newsworthy.

Step 4: How to Write Your Press Release

Now that we've covered the basics, it's time to get into the nuts and bolts of how to write a press release.

You need to understand that what you write will most probably get changed by the editor or journalist assigned to your article. Regardless, the idea is to include as much detail as possible. The easier you make the journalist's job, the greater your chance of success. So let's look at each component of a press release.

Headlines

The most important part of the press release is the headline. This is where you either sell your idea to the journalist, or you have your article thrown in the bin. We'll cover more about writing effective headlines later on, but for the moment we'll stick to the basics.

Your headline needs to be big, and it needs to grab attention. If you've never written one before, look at a few newspapers and magazines to get a feel. If you're writing one for the broadcast media, you'll need to approach it slightly differently. However, the principles will be the same.

Typefaces

The typeface or font you use can also make a big difference.

Basically, there are two types: sans serif and serif fonts. Sans serif fonts don't have the little "feet" at the bottom of each letter. Studies have shown that people find these fonts far more difficult to read than serif fonts. Serif fonts have the little "feet," which appear to form a line under the words that your eye can follow.

If you want a journalist to read your press release, I suggest you use serif fonts.

Point Size

The size of the font you use is referred to as the point size. Studies have shown readership doesn't drop off between 14 and 7 point size. But as a general rule, 10 point is ideal.

Highlighting Text

You should never highlight text in a press release. Don't use bold and never underline any part of it. And don't use *all capitals.* The only exception is in your headline, and then only if it's common practice for the publication you're sending it to.

To make the text easier to use, break it up into paragraphs, one thought to a paragraph. Block your first paragraph, and then indent subsequent ones.

Subheadlines

Once again, a press release is completely different than a print advertisement. You should not use subheadlines in your press release. Stick to using standard paragraphs.

Lead

The lead paragraph is all-important. It's where your press release will succeed or fail. If you've written an effective headline, the editor or reporter who's looking over your work will normally make a decision based on this paragraph.

As I mentioned earlier, this paragraph should not be indented. It should be roughly 60 words or less in length. That's all. Because this isn't very long, you must make every word count. What an editor will normally be looking for is the backbone of your story. The editor will generally want to know who is doing what, why, and where the event will take place.

It's imperative that you cover these points in your opening paragraph. Once again, if you're unsure about how to go about writing your opening few lines, read a number of publications to get a better understanding of what they like. If you're writing for a broadcast medium, you need to make your opening statement "punchy" and to the point. Using a quote, which encompasses the "nuts and bolts" of your story, can help you get your story aired.

Most journalists will edit from the bottom up, therefore any points you want to get across should be packed into the first paragraph. By placing them near the top of your press release, there's a greater chance they'll get mentioned.

Body Copy

This is the part where you expand on your lead paragraph. But by expand, I don't mean ramble on. You need to stick to the facts and keep it interesting. In the body of your press release, you need to explain what's special or unique about your product or service.

Remember, it has to be something worthwhile. Just because something is important to you doesn't mean it's important to somebody else. If you're selling a new product, explain what it does for the users and how it operates. If it has any unusual features, then this is the time to mention them.

The body copy is also the place where you should use any quotes you may have. But only use quotes if they're relevant. Don't use them just because you liked what someone said about you unless it's important to the story.

Make sure that if you've quoted another source, you explain clearly who or what that source is and, if possible, how the editor can verify those facts. Newspapers will take a very dim view of anyone who "alters" the facts, particularly if it results in their getting sued. Always make sure you have a way of proving what you say.

Your press release should tell a story and be easy to read. When you finish writing it, get someone to look it over and critique it for you. Ask yourself seriously if anyone else would find it newsworthy.

Sending press releases to the media is not the sort of thing you should do week in and week out. If you send in too many uninteresting article ideas, chances are when you actually have a good one, it'll get ignored. So if it isn't honestly interesting, don't send it in.

Some Basic Considerations

Whenever you write a press release, there are seven fundamental rules you must follow.

1. Always type the words "PRESS RELEASE" across the top of the page. This makes it easier for members of the newsroom to identify what it is so they can work out who it should go to. Unlike the body of your press release, these words should be set in all caps.

2. Include the date. This should be the date you sent the press release. In the case of a late-breaking news item, you should also include the time. If you want the press release be used right away, type "**FOR IMMEDIATE RELEASE**" in bold caps immediately under the date. If, however, you want to give the media advanced warning of an impending launch, for instance, but you don't want them to run with the story until a particular date, then type the words "**EMBARGOED UNTIL**" in bold caps under the date.

3. Double space lines. The journalists who are working on your story will need space to make notes. By leaving enough space between the lines, you'll make it easier for them to do just that. It's a good idea to leave wide margins for the same reason.

4. Put all the key points at the top of the page. As I've mentioned previously, when journalists edit stories, they'll generally do it from the bottom up. Understanding this, there's no point building up to a grand finale. Put anything you definitely want included in the article at the top. This way you'll ensure that they have a better chance of not being altered.

5. Check spelling. Because members of the newsroom tend to be busy, they won't want to spend time correcting your spelling. Make sure the names of all people and places are spelled correctly. It's always a good idea to have someone proofread it for you before you send it.

6. Stick to the facts. Although it is said that reporters stretch the truth a little, they do take a very dim view of anything that isn't factual. For this reason, it's important that you don't try to make a story out of nothing. This will make the reporter look foolish and could backfire on you because it'll quash any hope you may have had of getting anything printed in the future. Worse still, the reporter may even keep a close eye on you, hoping for an opportunity to give you some negative publicity when the opportunity arises.

7. Include your name and contact details. Although this may seem obvious, the number of people who make this unforgivable mistake would surprise you. Journalists often work shifts or unusual hours, so make sure you supply them with all necessary numbers and the times during which you can be contacted. If a journalist needs extra information but can't track you down, your press release will end up in the trash.

Pictures

If you've got an upcoming event you're publicizing, and you think it will be newsworthy from a photographic point of view, type the words **PHOTO OPPORTUNITY** in bold caps at the end of your press release. Then outline what you think will make a good, newsworthy photograph. It could be a famous personality who will be available for the media to photograph. Give the details— time, place, whom to contact, and what the scenario is. Once again, the event must be newsworthy. You may have a hot air balloon display in your parking lot or a famous celebrity in your store. That would certainly be something the local media would be interested in.

If you believe you have something worth taking a photograph of, contact your local paper and find out who is in charge of that department. In smaller papers this will normally be the editor, but large papers may have specialist photography editors.

If you're taking the photographs yourself, you need to make sure that they are clear and focused. Try not to get posts or other obstacles in the way of your subject. Although the production department of the newspaper will be able to scan the photograph into a computer and then tidy it up, they won't want to spend a lot of time fixing your mistakes.

By getting the shot right the first time, you'll improve your chances of getting it published. It's also a good idea to take a number of shots from different angles. Send a few to the paper so the editor has a choice.

Always put a caption on the back of your photograph. Include your name and contact details because photos often get separated from press releases.

Urgency

You may need to make your press release sound urgent. To do this, simply place **"FOR IMMEDIATE RELEASE"** at the top under the date. You may also get a good result from offering an exclusive to a particular publication or media outlet. In this situation, explain that the story you've sent won't be sent to anyone else for a specified period of time.

The length of time obviously depends on which form of media you're dealing with. For example, there'd be no point holding off for 24 hours after the story has been aired on the local television station. The benefit here is the fact that the story will be seen on TV before anyone hears about it on the radio. The media is very competitive, so offering one TV station a "scoop" might just be what it is after. Newspapers tend to deal more with recent happenings because of printing deadlines.

Contacting the Right Person

Writing a good press release is really only half the battle. You need to ensure that it gets to the right person. By calling the newspaper or station in advance, you can identify whose responsibility it is to look after stories in your field. For example, if you were organizing a sporting event, you wouldn't send your press release to the lifestyle editor. Find out who you need to speak to, and then give her a brief outline of your story idea. Don't take up too much of her time. Unless she wants to interview you over the phone, simply tell her you're sending through a press release, and that she should look out for it.

Also point out that you'll call back to make sure it's been received. When you call back, don't simply say that you're calling to make sure she received your press release; you need to take advantage of this opportunity to "sell" her on the idea of the story. Give her more information that perhaps you haven't covered in the original press release, or mention any photo opportunities that may arise.

When dealing with radio or television stations, you'll probably be sending information to the program director or the individual host or announcer. Unless you know him well, you're better off mailing or faxing your press release to him. The exception is when you've got a hot story that is happening as you speak. In this situation, you're better off phoning in the story. For example, you may have a huge crowd trying to get into your store to take advantage of a special sale. In this instance, you'd call the station with the angle that traffic is being interrupted due to the success of the sale.

If you're sending your press release to a newspaper, the situation is slightly different. You should call the paper in advance to find out whom it is the press release should be addressed to, as more often than not, you'll be dealing directly with a reporter rather than with the editor.

Once you've identified the correct journalist, send your information through and follow up on the phone. But only do it with worthwhile stories. If you're sending through a standard, general press release, don't bother following up; it just makes them mad.

Finding Out What Works

When you've finished writing your press release, it's time to test and measure. Test your headline and appeal by sending it and measuring the response it receives. Unlike advertisements, you can't run the same press release week after week and expect it to work each time. The best way to test your headline and appeal is to send it to a publication or media outlet that isn't the one you're really after.

To explain what I mean, consider this hypothetical situation. You have a story of an upcoming event in your business, and you'd like it to run in a large daily newspaper. Before sending it to that paper, you might try sending it to a smaller, weekly publication to test the response. If the smaller paper likes your idea and wants to do a story, then chances are the larger paper will like it as well. If it doesn't, then go back to the drawing board and start again.

You're best off not sending exactly the same press release to different newspapers in the same area. Although most papers will edit and change the story, some may simply print your story as is. It would be embarrassing for all concerned if the same story appeared word for word in two different papers.

Step 5: How Long Should Your Press Release Be?

Keep your press release to one page if at all possible. If you've ever seen the insides of a typical newsroom, you understand why. With papers strewn from one end of the office to the other, and people running all over the place, pages get lost. If a journalist can find only one page of your two-page fax, guess what happens to your story? That's right; it's dumped in the trash again.

If you can't fit everything you need to cover onto one page, you may wish to mail your press release instead of faxing it. By doing this, you'll be able to staple the pages together so they don't get lost. This, of course, works only with stories that are not urgent.

If your story is urgent, and you can't fit it on one page, write the word "MORE" at the bottom of page one. Then start your next page with the heading, "Page two of (whatever your original headline was)."

Remember, journalists are busy and don't want to read a novel. If your press release looks more like an epic saga, you'll need to trim it down. Remember, much of what you need to say can be covered in a later interview or phone call.

Step 6: When to Run Your Press Release

If your product is perennial (that is, not seasonal), you don't have to be too concerned about when to distribute your press release. You see, unless you're publicizing an event that has a definite date, or the launch of a product that has a definite launch date, you're very much in the hands of the media.

Sure, send your press release, but you can't really expect to see it run on a particular day. After all, it is free publicity you're aiming for. Unlike paid advertising when you certainly do get to choose when your ad runs, it's very different with press releases. When they give it a run (if they do) depends on so many uncontrollable variables like newsworthiness, what else is happening, timeliness, space, and general interest.

Step 7: What Else Do You Need to Think About?

Use this section as a final checklist. Once you're happy with your press release, run through and make sure you're ready to get started. Here are a few things you may not have thought about:

Phone Scripts: There are hundreds of cases where an article has made the phone ring off the hook, but the business owner saw very few sales at the end of the day. It's all to do with "conversion"—that is, how many inquiries were turned into sales. You need a script—a version of what you say to encourage people to buy. Just think about the best sales lines you've ever used, and compile them into one typed script. Make sure you ask lots of "open-ended questions"—questions that start with who, what, where, why, etc. Give a copy to every member of your team and make sure they *use* it.

And, of course, make sure your team members know that an article may be appearing soon and that they should *expect* calls.

Check Stock and Staff Levels: It's unlikely your article will bring in hundreds of people (very few actually do), but you need to be prepared for a sizable response. There would be nothing worse than having a rush of customers, then running out of stock. Or being too busy to service the new leads that the press release generated. Plan for the publication of the article, and make sure you can cater to any increased demand that may result.

Angles

What Works and What Doesn't

So you've written a great headline and an exciting first paragraph. But what are you going to say to get your press release printed? Contacting the relevant person and laying your press release out the right way will not in itself assure you of success. You need to find a unique and interesting angle.

So What Is a Great Angle?

When thinking of what angle to use, ask yourself this: "Is this the sort of story I would read or want to listen to?"

If the answer is "no," then go back to the drawing board. Without a great angle, you cannot achieve great results.

An important thing to consider when deciding on the correct angle is whether or not publication of the press release will still suit your needs. For example, you may be able to find a very interesting angle about a new product, but can you word your press release in such a way that it will bring you sales? Although I've already mentioned that a press release is not free advertising space, you still need to get your company's name up there for it to be of any value to you. So let's have a look at some interesting angles.

Types of Angles

Here are some possible angles that would be worth considering.

Celebration

Stories about celebrations may not always be considered "newsworthy." For example, if your store is celebrating its 20th birthday, you would not expect the same coverage as you would if you were having your 50th birthday.

The best way to get some exposure for your celebrations is to have an event or promotion that is out of the ordinary. Maybe get a sports figure to visit your store, or have demonstrations by industry experts in-store. Remember, if you don't have anything exceptional to shout about, you can't expect to get much, if any, in the way of news coverage.

To give you an idea of the sort of celebrations that would generate interest, consider a store that's having a one-millionth customer's bonus. The store may already have had more than 990,000 customers come through its doors. Now if the only people who know the exact number that have come through are the storeowners, there will be an amount of suspense built up around when the one-millionth customer arrives.

The trick here is to have a sensational bonus for the lucky customer who becomes customer number 1,000,000. For example, if you owned a supermarket, you might consider giving that person 12 months of free groceries. Other worthwhile examples could be an around-the-world trip, or a new luxury car.

You need to understand the higher the dollar value of the prize, the more exposure you're likely to get.

Also keep in mind the possibility of getting other companies or suppliers to come in on the deal with you. For example, you might contact a local travel agent with your idea of giving away an around-the-world trip. You could explain to the agent how much exposure this could give her business. This way you get to offset the cost of running the promotion, and you get to offer prizes that might otherwise be out of the question.

Once you have worked out what you're giving away, you need to contact the media outlets that you want to target. Send them a press release and a fact sheet to let them know what you're doing, and what it is you're offering. Try to get them to run a story to let people know the prize should be won sometime next month.

I would not suggest you have them run the story any more than four weeks from the time you expect the prize to be won, otherwise they'll look silly and the public will get sick of waiting.

It is then advisable to warn them on the day that the prize is likely to be won. This will give them a chance to come to the store to photograph and interview the winner.

Remember that if you have an exceptional prize, you will get a lot more people through your store than would normally be the case. So if you typically have 1000 customers a day, you could expect to have two or even three times that amount during the promotion.

Keep this in mind when you're contacting the media. If it would normally take seven weeks to get that many customers through, once you've given it exposure, it may only take three or four weeks after the "hype" starts.

These are just a few examples of celebration ideas that would be of a newsworthy nature.

If you take some time to consider the possibilities, and put a bit of effort into coming up with good prizes and promotions, you're sure to be onto a winner.

Specific Interest Groups

If you're targeting a specific interest group through a specialist publication, such as motorcycle riders through a motorcycle magazine, then you're almost certain to get some coverage, providing your story is newsworthy.

Even if you don't have a specialist magazine to target, you can usually get some worthwhile exposure in your local media, particularly if the media has sections devoted to the subject. But once again you have to be promoting something out of the ordinary. New product launches, a special guest at your store (the more famous the better), or a demonstration day are all things worth covering.

A good example of this is a boating and fishing store looking to run a weekend promotion to increase store traffic. Now if it planned its weekend well in advance, there would be a good chance it could organize a very successful, and newsworthy, promotion. The first thing it would need to consider is the type of demonstrations or events that would get people excited.

The business should start by contacting its suppliers and getting them to pitch in with displays and new product demonstrations. Not only would these suppliers be required to set up display stands and new products, they'd also need to have experts on site to answer questions and demonstrate how the new products work.

If the business plays its cards right, it'll also have new boats and motors on display. It should also have life jackets and safety gear, as well as stalls set up by any government bodies responsible for licensing and safety. This would give customers a chance to find out what fishing and boating licenses they need, as well as giving the governing authorities the chance to get "on the same page" with the public.

Of course, having the latest in fishing rods, reels, and tackle would get people into the store and create a fair amount of interest.

Now you might say, "Yeah, that sounds like a great idea. They'd have to get media coverage for a weekend like that." But the chances are the business probably won't receive much exposure, if any. You see, the problem is that none of the things I've mentioned are headline material. Sure they're worth having there, and people may be eager to come along, but can you see any of them making a good headline? I mean honestly, how lame would it be to have a headline like "Boating laws explained at Joe Bloggs' Fishing Expo?"

You see, all Joe Bloggs has is a good start. But it needs a draw card, something you wouldn't normally get to see, something the media could really sink its teeth into.

The answer? A fish tank. No not your "run-of-the-mill," seen-in-every-home- and office fish tank. No, I mean one of those huge fish tanks that are set up on the back of a semitrailer. These tankers have sides that drop down so that you can see the fish swimming inside.

So what's the purpose of this fishing tanker? Well, I'm glad you asked. You see, companies use them to demonstrate how different lures and tackle work with different species of fish. They take the barbs off the hooks so the fish can swallow the lures, allowing them to come straight back out without causing any harm. These tankers will normally come complete with their own tents or marquees, so they don't take up any space inside the store.

Now, this sort of attraction would not only make a great headline, but would also present a fantastic photographic opportunity.

So, if you want to attract interest from a very specific or targeted market, make sure you have something worthwhile and newsworthy to secure yourself the type of exposure that's needed to make your promotion a success.

Tragedy/Fear

You need to be very careful when using this angle, as the wrong wording or emphasis could have a very adverse effect on your business. Having said that, it is also one of the most powerful angles when used to your advantage.

To give you an idea, let's take a look at a hypothetical press release written by a government health department regarding the dangers of parents not immunizing their children.

Now in this situation the department might consider talking about the tragic case of a small child dying unnecessarily from a disease that could have been avoided through immunization. Because this is a highly emotional story (most stories about suffering children are), it is more than newsworthy if put the right way. In this instance, the department needs to focus on the sadness and upset the parents are experiencing, simply because they did not fully understand the dangers involved in not having their children immunized.

Some people may feel this type of story plays too heavily on people's emotions. However, as you can no doubt see, a photograph of the grieving parents accompanied by the story of their loss would most likely get the desired result.

Fear also comes into play with this sort of angle. A good example would be in the case of new taxation laws. Imagine a press release from an accounting firm that explained, in layman's terms, the possible consequences resulting from the new tax regulations. It could point out that people who haven't protected themselves against these changes could find themselves being heavily fined. Most people, being scared of losing their hard-earned savings, would most probably be spurred into action. But it needs to be carefully worded to demonstrate that the particular accounting firm that posted the release knows how to safeguard against the ramifications of the new changes.

By carefully choosing your words and placing the correct emphasis on your story, you'll find fear and tragedy can bring some amazing results. But remember, it's focusing on a negative, and that can occasionally backfire.

Family Appeal

A safer type of angle is one that focuses on a positive, particularly one involving family interest and children. You see, everyone likes hearing happy and humorous stories about children, but you need to remember that you're not trying to do the journalist out of a job; you're trying to increase your sales and store traffic.

For this type of press release, you might consider talking about how or why you sponsor a local children's sports team. Or maybe you've made a donation to a worthwhile charity after posting record profits. The whole idea here is to get people thinking about your business in a positive way.

To give you a more specific idea, imagine a retail store that was concerned about the high unemployment and poverty levels in its community. Now if it was doing a Christmas appeal where for every $10 spent in December, it would donate $1 to a worthwhile Christmas charity, it would be reasonable to expect some amount of media attention.

The store might even have a Christmas tree set up where people could leave donations for underprivileged children. However, it's all been done before and many companies are jumping in on the Christmas bandwagon.

But imagine if a retail store did a similar promotion in May. If the store wrote a press release that spoke about the hardships faced by these families all year round, and the fact that people seemed to forget that Christmas is not the only time they struggle, we'd have a whole new angle.

Store employees could start up a winter program where they would donate money or goods to struggling families in the region. People could buy food items, bedding, or clothing from the store at a discounted price if they were donating the items to this worthy cause.

Or maybe they could have a bonus dollar system where the bonus dollars could be converted into donations. A story like this, accompanied by a photo of a cold and lonely child, could bring an amazing response from the community.

But it doesn't have to be this dramatic. It could be as simple as organizing a fingerpainting or poetry competition for children in your store. With a bit of imagination, you're sure to find a story that will have people thinking about your company in a warm and positive way.

These are just a few of the many angles that'll lead to your press release's being printed or going to air. But regardless of which one you choose, it's important to realize you must have a worthwhile or newsworthy angle if your press release is to be successful.

The Wrap-Up

So there you have it—the system for writing press releases that will hopefully generate extra business for you and your company. But there are a few things you need to keep in mind before you send out your first batch.

Remember, your story must be honest and accurate if you want it to be published. Journalists and reporters hate to be made fools of. It also has to be newsworthy if it's to get the desired reception when you submit it. Don't waste the time of the newsroom, or editorial department, with something that has no real appeal.

Technology has made it is possible to submit press releases via e-mail. In fact, I would say that the majority of media outlets around the country already offer this service. The advantage here for the journalist, of course, is ease of editing because it wouldn't need to be retyped. It would probably pay to contact your local papers, radio, and TV stations, to ask how they prefer having press releases submitted.

Bradley J. Sugars

It's also important to have a good relationship with the media centers in your area. Taking the local editors and news managers out to lunch is a good start. It would also pay to give them a bit of a discount when they come into your store. It doesn't have to be much, but it pays to remember that many of them have large egos so it's the thought, rather than the savings, that counts.

Another thing you might want to consider is the possibility of writing a regular column for your local paper, or maybe having a time slot on one of the local stations. If you believe you have something to offer in this regard, put together a proposal and submit it to the relevant people. You see, if it's newsworthy and would create interest, why wouldn't they run with it? For example, a computer store could run a weekly technology column. Or maybe you could try for a 10-minute spot on a radio talk show.

To succeed with this type of promotion, you need to convince the station or paper of the ongoing benefits. To do this, list a number of potential topics you'd like to discuss, and maybe even write the first three or four complete articles as examples of what you can do. Then explain to the media outlet that you're not after any financial return; instead you're simply interested in getting some exposure for yourself and your business.

There are some things to be mindful of, however. For starters, you can't keep mentioning your company's name. Sure it's all right to mention it on the odd occasion. After all, if you couldn't mention your business, what's the point of going to all the effort in the first place? But you can't appear to be biased. You need to speak objectively and simply about the relevant topics or issues.

Having said that, there's nothing wrong with reviewing a product and then mentioning that it's available in your store.

Another thing to remember is that your article or time slot is no place to have a shot at your competitors. Not only will you come across as being less than objective, it will also lead to your being taken "off the air" or having your column discontinued.

Another point that's closely related is one of moral values and personal beliefs. The readers or listeners have their own personal views and beliefs and don't need you shoving yours down their throats. Keep to the facts and everyone will be happy.

Next you'll find examples along with an explanation of other documents used in the field of public relations. By combining the knowledge you now have with these examples, you should have every chance of success with your press releases.

Press Releases and Supporting Documents

Press releases aren't the only types of documents you can send to the media. As I said earlier, it's important to keep your documents brief and to the point. Sending too many pages can be a waste of time, as some of them can become lost in the clutter of the average newsroom. In any case, many journalists are just too busy to spend all day wading through your information.

Having said that, there are a number of supporting documents you can send to help get your story covered. These documents are designed to give editors all the information they need when deciding whether or not to send a reporter out to cover your promotion. Here's how each one works:

Press Releases

A press release is basically a story you send to the media. It's written in such a way that it could go straight into print. It's designed to be a "ready-to-go" article that a journalist could edit or rework into a larger article if need be.

Fact Sheets

A fact sheet, as the name implies, gives journalists all the facts they'll need when preparing to cover your story. You simply list on a page, in bullet-point form, all the points of interest concerning your story. Journalists find this additional information invaluable, as it gives them something to base their questions on. It also gives you an opportunity to ensure that points you want covered in the article get mentioned.

To give you an idea of what a fact sheet could contain, consider the case of a store that is running a weekend promotion. If it has competitions running over the course of the weekend, it could list the types of competitions, who the judges are, the prizes that are offered, and when each competition is to be judged or drawn.

Bradley J. Sugars

If the store also had a sports figure appearing live in store, the fact sheet would explain who the celebrity is. It would also list the times that person is going to actually be there and when he would be available for interviews. It would not go into too much detail about the athlete's history and achievements; that would be covered in a media advisory.

Media Advisory

A media advisory is similar in some ways to a fact sheet. The major difference, however, is that it's designed to "sell" the journalist on the idea of covering your event.

To give you an idea of what I mean by "sell," let's take a look at our hypothetical weekend promotion again.

The media advisory would list things such as photographic and story opportunities. By suggesting story angles, and offering ideas on the types of photographs that could be taken, it attempts to convince the media's decision makers that it's a newsworthy event.

It would also give the journalist some facts and figures to base their report on. For example, if Robert Johnson, the world's fastest sprinter, were to appear in store, it would list his major career highlights and any upcoming events he will be competing in. If the store is located in a small, country town, and Robert himself came from a similar town, it could list similarities between the two towns.

In many cases, the athlete's manager will have already supplied this information to you. If not, simply ask for it, and explain that you're looking to have the event covered by the media.

It's extremely unlikely that the manager will say "no," as he realizes the only way to charge the huge sums of money for guest appearances is by getting the store more exposure through the media.

Teaser Letters

Sometimes referred to as "pitch letters," a teaser letter is normally sent out prior to the event. It should be short and to the point, listing what it is you hope to do.

It should give the editor an idea of any newsworthy stories, photographic opportunities, and potential guest appearances.

These letters are not designed to give the whole story, but simply to let the relevant people know that a good story opportunity could be coming up. It has the advantage of getting the media interested, so when you send your press release, the media has a sense of "Oh, that's the story I've been waiting on." But remember to keep these letters very brief. They are not designed to tell the story, but merely to whet the appetite.

"So, there you have it, Charlie—all you need to know about press releases. What do you think?"

"Man, that's powerful stuff, Brad. But how can I use it? I mean, I'm only a small garage owner. What could I possibly say that the media would find newsworthy?"

"There's a whole heap of things. You just need to sit down and think about it. But I'm sure I don't need to tell you that. I can see you have an idea already."

"What I'm thinking is this: I could have a campaign, but before the start of the school holiday period, where I promote car safety. The idea is to get drivers to pop in for a free safety check, then if something is uncovered, I get to do the work for them. How's that sound?"

"Terrific. Now, how about drafting a press release to publicize it?"

Charlie was no writer, but as he went along making changes and corrections, his draft slowly began to take shape. It wasn't long before he was satisfied enough to show it to me.

"Great work, Charlie. This is really good, especially for your very first attempt."

I read through it again. He was a quick learner.

This is what he had written:

PRESS RELEASE

2/09/02

Parent's apathy puts children at risk

The disturbing number of children injured in cars each year is due largely to the fact that parents don't seem to care. According to Charlie, proprietor of a leading Brisbane mechanical workshop, many parents are risking their children's safety with a "she'll-be-all-right" attitude.

Charlie explained that approximately 5000 Australian children under the age of 5 are taken to the hospital each year with injuries sustained largely as a result of child restraints being incorrectly installed.

"People are just unaware of the dangers posed by installing child restraints incorrectly," Charlie said. "Very often they are fitted the wrong way, and that's the most worrisome thing of all, as this is a fundamental mistake to make."

Charlie said that these days there was no excuse for not having a child restraint, as prices had come down significantly over the past few years. "In the past, specialist suppliers were the only place where you could buy child restraints, but now that the major chain stores have begun stocking them, people are opting for the lower prices, but missing out on ensuring they are correctly installed by deciding to install them themselves. The result has been a huge increase in child injury rates."

Charlie explained that he would be campaigning for child safety this holiday season by offering free safety inspections.

"All you have to do is phone in for an appointment, and my team of trained technicians will check your child restraint for you, free of charge. And that's not all. Seeing as the car is in the workshop, we'll give it a free overall safety check as well."

Anyone interested can call Charlie's Garage at 321 1234.

Examples

Over the next two pages you'll find an example of a press release and a media advisory that have been designed to get noticed, get published, and attract more customers.

Keep in mind the information you've just learned and read through the examples carefully. It's a good idea to write the example out, word for word, so you become used to the style of writing that's required. Once you have the "feel" for it, try one of your own. You'll be surprised at just how easy it is.

PRESS RELEASE

Date
03/12/2005

Imported fashions cause stir in marketplace

Local clothing agent and manufacturer, Zebra Concepts, has just secured the rights to import two popular U.S. labels, it was announced yesterday by Zebra Marketing Director, Judy Alley.

"We're very excited. This is a real coup, not only for us but for Canadian fashion in general," Alley said. "Kerrie Craig and Regina Doolan are two of the most exclusive designer labels to come out of the United States. There's already a buzz around the marketplace since word of our success leaked out."

Well known in the New Zealand fashion industry for its innovative marketing, Alley puts the company's success down to well-developed strategies. "We've worked hard in recent times to be different," she said. "With the assistance of one of the leading U.S. marketing companies, *Action International*, we've begun to offer a number of revolutionary services to our clients."

Zebra Concepts provides a number of unique services for its customers. "We help them with such areas of marketing as using point-of-sale material, store layout, and window displays," said Alley. "We actually employ someone to go to each store and train our customers in these areas."

One of the most successful strategies is that of closed-door sales. "These sales take place after hours," explained Alley. "Stores invite their clients to exclusive previews of the upcoming season's fashions." Speaking with Alley, you soon realize why Zebra Concepts have become such a success. "Our philosophy is based on customer service," says Alley. "We believe that business is meant to be fun, and that a happy store is a successful store." Zebra Concepts can be contacted directly at (01) 234 5678.

Contact name: Judy Alley
Phone Number: (01) 234 5678

Media Advisory

Date
00/00/00

Zebra Concepts is about to launch two exclusive Australian brands into the New Zealand Market

Zebra Concepts is holding an invitation-only launch of its exciting new U.S. labels on Tuesday, starting at 7:00 p.m. The launch will be attended by a number of well-known celebrities and will feature some of Canada's most vibrant up-and-coming new models.

Your Contact: Judy Alley

Photographic Opportunities:

Exclusive previews of new labels.

Some of Canada's best young models.

A selection of well-known celebrities including actors, actresses, singers, and public figures.

The Event: Launch of exclusive new U.S. clothing labels

The Venue: The Mahogany Room, 123, Central Plaza Palace, Auckland.

The Date: Tuesday, March 24th.

The Time: 7:00 p.m. for drinks and finger foods. Show starts at 7:45 p.m.

PRESS RELEASE

Date
00/00/0000

Place Your Specific Interest-Group Heading Here

[Make your strongest statements in this paragraph. Remember that press releases are edited from the bottom up. You need to put the key information in this paragraph. No more than 60 words.]

[Write from this point on as if you're a reporter interviewing yourself about the story. Use your surname when referring to yourself. Start to mention the facts and figures in this paragraph.]

[This paragraph is a follow-up of the previous one. Here you get into even more detail, explaining the benefits of your service or product. You need to prove a difference in this paragraph. By that I mean you need to show why your product, service, or event is different than any others that are in the marketplace at the same time.]

[Continue on in this paragraph, as you have in the previous one. It is a good idea to look as if you're asking some tough questions here. But remember to ask only the questions that you have a good answer to. The easiest way to do this is to look for a reason why someone would not believe what you're saying, and then prove that what you're saying is correct.]

[In this section you need to tell people how they can get in touch with you. Remember to include a contact number for people to reach you. You might need to include after-hours numbers for the journalist who will be covering the story. Make sure that these do not get published if they're not for use by the general public.]

Part 2

▌Direct Mail

"What we're going to concentrate on now, Charlie, is direct mail. I'm going to show you how to write direct mail letters that generate a response and make you money."

"You're talking my language, Brad. Keep going."

"I'll show you exactly how to put together powerful sales letters that get read and acted upon. But before I get started, I want to again stress the importance of testing and measuring every step along the way. You see, there are no hard-and-fast rules to marketing. Much of it is trial and error. So, you try something out and measure the results you get. If they're not great, you fine-tune the idea, or design something different based on your results. It's essential that you meticulously record every result, and even though it means extra work, you'll really be glad you did, believe me."

I always stress the importance of testing and measuring because it really is so important. Do this, and half your battle is over.

"OK, Charlie, now I know you're familiar with the basic idea of direct mail, but even so, I'm going to go over the basics, as a good grounding is essential. It always is. You comfortable with that?"

"Absolutely, Brad. Keep talking."

What Is a Successful Direct Mail Campaign?

Some businesspeople have unrealistic expectations concerning the response they should get from the average direct mail campaign. They expect a response rate of between 75 percent and 80 percent, but the reality is that most campaigns only return a fraction of that. So what then should you expect? That all depends.

You see, there's no definitive answer here. Consider this: A real estate agency could mail 3000 letters to past clients about a new property it has just listed. It may receive only two phone calls as a result, both of which lead to inspections. But what if one of those prospective buyers actually bought a property? This direct mail campaign would certainly be considered very successful. It's not the ratio of responses to letters posted that determines success, but money earned in relation to what the campaign costs.

To put it in a nutshell, any direct mail campaign that pays for itself can be considered successful. So before embarking on any direct mail campaign there are a few things you need to understand:

1. **Work out your costs.** This includes the cost of printing, envelopes, any implements you put in the envelope, the cost of buying or acquiring a direct mail list, and obviously, the postage.

2. **Know your margins.** You need to know the net profit you make from anyone who buys your product or service. By understanding how much you actually make from each sale, you'll be able to work out the percentage response required to make your campaign profitable.

3. **Lifetime value.** Don't view each new customer your campaign brings in as a once-off sale. You will normally lose money on the first sale to a new client in any case. The average business will need to sell to a client two times before it begins to make a profit from it.

With this in mind, you need to focus on strategies aimed at bringing customers back on a regular basis. Therefore, any direct mail campaign that covers its cost initially will turn out to be profitable in the long term. A realistic response rate from the average campaign would be between 20 percent and 35 percent.

What Makes a Successful Direct Mail Campaign?

Understanding our aim is to achieve between 20 percent and 35 percent response to our campaign, we need to look at the individual components of that campaign. We'll deal with these one by one in a moment, but first we need to identify them individually.

Targeted Lists

You don't want to mail to anyone who wouldn't be interested in your product or service.

Headlines

This is the most important part of your direct mail letter. If it doesn't grab your readers' interest immediately, your campaign will fail.

Body Copy

Once your headline has gotten the attention of the reader, you need to convey the benefits of buying your product or services in a clear, believable, and easy-to-read fashion.

Objects

Putting items in with your letter can greatly improve your response rate. Things like mints, balloons, rubber bands, and tissues can all be used to make your letter stand out and increase the chances of its being read.

Envelope

This is the first thing your prospect will see. If you don't put some thought and effort into designing an effective envelope, chances are your letter won't even get opened.

Phone Script

Unless you're selling directly off the page, you need to have an effective follow-up phone script handy. This can mean the difference between a 9 percent and a 25 percent response rate.

In the following pages, you'll learn how to buy, or develop, a targeted list. You will be shown in easy-to-follow steps how to write effective headlines, how to structure your body copy for maximum impact, and the type of items you can include with your letter to increase its response rate.

You'll also discover the types of offers that get the phone running hot and those that don't. Plus I'll also give you practical tips on how to package your letter to make sure it avoids the trash can.

The Seven Steps to Writing Great Direct Mail Letters

Step 1: Why Use Direct Mail?

Before writing anything, you need to work out whether direct mail is for you. You might have a suspicion it is but need to compare its potential returns to other marketing tools. For example, if your market is broad and your offer is *very* appealing, why not use the newspaper instead—it's easier and probably a cheaper way to go.

Direct mail is ideal when you have a specific group of people you want to advertise to, and there is a way to reach them. Here's a perfect example—event management companies. They know who their target market is (businesses that hold regular functions and events), and they know how to reach them (look up their address and send them a letter). Direct mail is perfect for situations like this.

On the other hand, direct mail is probably inappropriate for a fast food outlet as the market is probably too broad (anyone looking for a quick, cheap meal at lunchtime) and it's hard to reach it through the mail—where would you find addresses if you don't know names?

Of course, direct mail is always ideal for follow-up strategies—that is, marketing to people you've already dealt with. Writing them a letter to say "please come back," or "here's our latest product," or "it's time for a service," or even just "thanks." Remember though, direct mail letters are very often thrown away. Simply sending a letter is no longer enough. If you're going to mail out letters, be prepared to follow up each one with a phone call.

Step 2: Who Is Your Target Market?

Before you even buy the envelopes for your direct mail campaign, you need to identify exactly whom it is you're trying to reach. Precisely who is your target market?

Failure to answer this question will cost you hundreds in wasted dollars and lead to a poor conversion rate. For example, imagine a company that sells in-ground swimming pools doing a mailing campaign to a block of high-rise rental apartments. To avoid costly mistakes, you need to know who your potential customers are before you start mailing your letters out.

Knowing your target market will also enable you to write in a way that your prospects will relate to. Using terms and phrases that are commonly used by them will greatly increase the effectiveness of your letters.

So let's get specific. Who are the people most likely to be interested in your product or service? Here are some guidelines:

Age: How old are they? Don't just say "all ages" or "a variety." We want to create a mental picture of your average customers. Think of an age that symbolizes most of them.

Sex: Are they male or female? "Half and half" is too broad. Practically every business is split one way or the other. Give it some real thought—which gender does business with you currently?

Income: How much do they make? Do they earn a great living, meaning that quality is the big issue, or are they scraping for every dollar, always looking for a deal? It's essential that you find this out.

Where do they live? Are they local, or do they come from miles around to deal with you? This will dictate how you communicate with them.

3. Where Do You Find a Suitable List?

Now that you've identified the "who," you need to find a way of reaching them. Although there are many lists available, not all will be targeted. There are basically three ways to acquire a direct mail list.

Buy one from a broker

This is a quick, but expensive, way to get a mailing list. Most brokers can provide you with lists that target particular geographic or demographic segments of the population. For example, you can buy a list that will give you the names and addresses of women aged between 30 and 55 with an income of over $40,000 per year and who live within a seven-mile radius of your store.

While brokers can provide you with very specific lists, they tend to be far more expensive than general lists. Cost will normally dictate how targeted you can be when buying a list from these companies.

Mail to someone else's list

Find noncompetitive companies with similar target markets to yours. Then simply ask if you could mail to their list or if you could include your letter with one of their upcoming mailouts.

The success of this strategy relies on having a good relationship with the businesses in question. Although this method can be hit-or-miss, it can also be a very inexpensive way of reaching potential customers.

Create your own

This is one of the fastest and most effective ways to put together a list of people who are interested in your product or service.

The quickest way to compile your own list is to run a contest. To enter, people simply write their names and addresses on the entry forms provided and then drop them in a box. By offering one of your products or services as the prize, you have a greater chance of reaching only those people who are genuinely interested in what you have to sell.

To set up this contest you need to have tickets printed and a venue to run it in. Approach a shopping center, sporting club, or retail outlet and ask if the organization will let you leave your tickets and entry box on its premises.

Alternatively, you can run it as a "cut-out-the-coupon" contest in the local paper. If the prize you offer is of a high enough dollar value, the paper may run it free of charge. Contact the paper's promotions manager and explain your idea. You'll need to stress the interest the competition is going to create and how it will increase the paper's circulation.

Step 4: What Do You Want to Say to Your Prospects?

There's often heated debate about which type of direct mail letters work best, but there's never a disagreement about which type don't—those with no obvious purpose.

For example, if you write a letter that says, "Hi. My name's Harry. I cut hair, I've been doing it for 12 years," it's unlikely people will call. Your letter needs to give them a good reason to read it, then a great reason to do something about dealing with you.

Your letter needs to have a clear purpose, and it needs to take people from point A to point B.

Point A is your headline, which should identify where they are now. The body of the letter leads them to Point B, which is where you tell them why they should act right now, and how to do it.

It's most important to understand your customers. If you understand their needs, wants, and current situation, you can sell almost anything to them. For instance, mailing a letter to 47-year-old women with a headline that says, "Concerned about menopause? Here's why you don't need to be," could yield excellent results.

Or what about a letter to 17-year-olds that says, "Forget the fake ID—here's how you can get access to Sydney's best nightclubs before your 18th birthday." Or how about a letter to struggling musicians that says, "Tired of people passing your talent by? Here's how to take the bull by the horns and get famous—within 14 months."

These letters reach out and speak to the people reading them. If you don't understand the people you're writing to, you'll inevitably get off on the wrong foot with them. Imagine sending a letter to new mothers that says, "Is your baby bored? Here's why you should take your little one to Dreamworld." Your readers would be downright confused—anyone who's ever had a child wishes for a moment of peace, not more excitement.

Before writing anything, you need to decide exactly what message you want to communicate. You then need to decide what you want the recipients of your letter to do about it.

Here's a great example. Harry, the hairdresser, decides to write a letter to his past customers. Considering the abysmal result of his past "Hi, my name's Harry" letters, he resolves to get more specific. This time he has a clear message. You see, he has a new automatic rebooking system that makes life easier and saves his clients 20 percent. He also has some specific objectives—to encourage customers to use the new system, and to book for a haircut within the next two weeks.

Now the letter has a good chance of working.

It pays to remember that simply asking people to act now (or for that matter, telling them to act now) is rarely enough. You need to give them a good reason why *now* is the time to do something.

See, most purchases can be delayed forever. It's one thing to create desire, but it's another to actually get people to part with their cash. Every month, customers have to decide what to spend their money on. It could very realistically be a decision between buying a lovely oriental statuette, and buying the kids school shoes.

Every buyer has priorities. Of course, there are ways to rearrange these priorities.

If you offer a special deal on the statuette, the customer may think, "Well, the kids can wear those ratty sneakers a little longer, but I won't get this deal on this statuette again."

The question is, how do you offer a great deal without slicing your profit margin drastically? There's a couple of ways. First, make sure you are selling products or services that have a high margin. Often, that's not possible—try getting a high margin on gasoline. If you have the option of gearing your business towards higher-margin items, do so, as it'll make it much easier to come up with great deals.

If you can't do that, you need to find items or services that are highly valued by the customer, yet have a low cost. Extra service is an old standby; information booklets are another. Better still are services you can get for free from other businesses. For example, a hairdressing salon could offer to introduce its clients to a beauty salon if the beauty salon agrees to give every customer a free facial.

You'll find more details and examples of offers in Part 6.

Step 5: How Will You Write a Letter That Works?

It's a common misconception that you have to be a great writer, or some wizard with words, to write a letter that works.

That's rubbish. Some of the most successful letters have simply been written by people who know the people they're writing to, and who know how to come up with a good offer. Their writing skills are irrelevant.

Simply going to a database containing the names and addresses of stressed-out executives and saying, "100 percent less stress in 10 minutes or it's free . . . guaranteed. Normally $15, we come to you. Phone 4563 4525 for a *free* introductory session" is enough. It doesn't matter what language you use, or even if you make spelling mistakes. It might sound funny, but most people won't even notice. At the end of the day, people won't buy from you just because you can't write letters that are good enough to be published as poetry. By the same token, people probably won't avoid buying from you just because you can't spell "quixotic," "superfluous," or "rhetorical."

As long as your message is clear, quick, and well-targeted, your letter will work. It's really like serving food; if you're serving a delicious meal, it'll taste just as good delivered on paper plates as it will on your best china. People may prefer it on the china, but if you're serving to people hungry for what you've cooked, they'll eat anyway.

There is only one sin you don't want to commit—getting off the point, or rambling on for too long. If every word and every sentence says something important, fine. If your letter is full of guff, people will lose interest very quickly. The same applies if you stray from your initial intention and message.

Here Are Some More Guidelines

Your Headline

Tell people exactly what they will get from reading the letter. The headline lets prospects know whether they should bother reading on. It needs to promise immediate benefits. For example, "Here's how to make $4500 extra income this month (just by sleeping in two hours later)," or "Save 56% on your insurance bill."

The other approach is to invoke curiosity. This is harder to do effectively, but better if your product doesn't contain a striking benefit. Here's a good example: "Here's why three out of four children don't get enough calcium," or "Four reasons why you should jump for joy this week."

Most importantly, your headline needs to stop readers dead in their tracks. Another trick is to speak directly to them in your headline. For example, why not make your headline read something like, "George, here's how you can make an extra $19,000 this year and make Harriet happy."

If you have your customers' first names, this is easy to do with computer software.

Create a Strong Introduction

The first couple of sentences are incredibly important. They tell people whether they should read on in depth or start skimming. Nine out of 10 times they'll skim (or trash the letter entirely).

Here are a couple of powerful introductions that help get a higher readership:

"Before you start skimming, just stop. Stop and think about where your life is heading."

Or

"You don't know it yet, but the next five paragraphs contain the secret to earning a fortune, without breaking your back."

You need to immediately let people know they're doing the right thing by reading. Here's another "cut them off at the pass" style introduction:

"I know you're tempted to throw this letter away without reading it, but I have a warning for you."

Of course, in most cases your first paragraph will just support your headline. For example, "You're probably a little disbelieving. In fact, I'm certain you think I'm pulling your leg, but let me show you why that headline is 100 percent true."

Include a strong, specific call to action. If you don't tell people what to do, they probably won't do anything.

Give them precise instructions: Whom to call, which number to use, when to do it, and what to ask for. Here's a good example: "Call Gordon Harris now at 555-4567 and ask for your 45-page personal astrological analysis chart."

Better still, tell them to act, and then mention that you'll be phoning in the next couple of days to discuss the letter and offer further. Include concise and convincing body copy. This is the actual text between the introduction and the call to action. You don't need to be a great writer to do this part well. It's more important that you get the point across clearly, in as few words as possible, and in logical order.

After you write your first draft, go through and edit it viciously. Cut out any sentence or word that doesn't need to be there. Next, read it aloud and make sure it flows. Then have a couple of people check it through, and ask them to tell you what they got out of it. Ask them to explain it back to you, just to make sure you're getting the point across. Ask which parts were boring, and don't be afraid of criticism. You didn't set out to be the world's greatest writer anyway, so any comments should be helpful, rather than hurtful.

Subheadlines

If your letter is a long one (by this I mean anything over two pages), it's important to break your text up with subheadlines. These are short miniheadlines that guide the readers through the letter and pique their interest.

There's nothing wrong with making each one as attractive as your main headline.

Use a P.S.

One of the most important aspects of the copy is the P.S. In fact, the P.S. is often the most read part of the letter. P.S. is an abbreviation for "postscript" and is used to add an additional point at the end of a letter. It pays to include a major point right at the end. For example, list an extra special bonus if the offer is taken up in the next three days.

People tend to read the P.S. because it's unexpected. They're surprised that someone has forgotten to include something. Some professional copywriters use up to three or four P.S.'s and write up to half a page for each. It sounds crazy, but it seems to work.

Make the Layout "Fun"

When writing your letter, forget everything you learned in school about writing a "business letter."

Indent paragraphs, splash bold throughout, use bullet points, and give everything lots of space. If you look at your letter and think, "My gosh, that's a lot," you need to take another look at your layout. Perhaps it needs to be spread out. Or maybe you need to take out a paragraph and put its main points in bullet form.

Watch Out for Letters That Are Too Long or Too Short

The number of pages is less important than the actual layout. If spacing it out spills the letter over onto three pages rather than one, that's OK—just as long as it looks "fun" to read.

There's a common perception that a one-page letter will always be read. There's some truth in this, but there's also a lot of mistruth mixed in there too. If the letter is packed solid with text just so it'll fit on one page, people will be more turned off than if it were four pages and spaced.

Likewise, if it's uninteresting and untargeted, people won't read it out of politeness. And if it doesn't have enough meat and reasons to act, people won't do anything. You need to say enough to get them inspired to do something, but not so much that they run out of time, or get bored.

Avoid Anything That's Hard to Read

Type your letter in a standard serif or sans serif font: Times New Roman or Courier. While another funny font may look nicer, it'll be hard to read. Remember, people aren't interested in playing games by trying to decipher your bizarre typeface. They just want to know if they should bother reading, and if they like what they read, what they should do.

Don't make things confusing; it'll only obscure your message. And avoid being an artist. Be a businessperson instead.

Include a Gimmick

The very best direct mail letters contain some sort of gimmick, something out of the ordinary that makes them memorable and interesting. Here are a few examples:

A letter headed, "Here's why life is sweeter when you're with MGA Insurance," included a lollipop.

A piece of salami was sent with a letter. The tie-in was that one rotten piece could bring down a whole company. At the time, the "salami incident" (where a piece of salami allegedly poisoned and killed a young girl, subsequently destroying the company) was still fresh in the minds of the readers. The letter was for an employment agency that helped you weed out the "rotten apples."

Forty cents was taped to the top of a letter, the headline of which was, "I'm so eager to show you the new line of Grubic Motorcycles, I've already paid for you to call me."

A small bag of fertilizer was mailed with a letter to agricultural wholesalers. The headline was, "Here's 30 grams of our most advanced fertilizer. Here's why you'll soon need 30 tons of the stuff."

A gimmick is a brilliant way to get attention, and to stop people in their tracks. It's also great if you're following up your letter with a phone call. Imagine calling after mailing the letter with the piece of salami. Instead of the usual "Oh, I don't know. I may have read it" reply, you'd get "Oh, that letter."

Envelope

There's mixed opinion on whether you should write anything on the envelope. People will open anything in a plain white envelope with their names on it—it could be a bill, a notice from the government, or a check. Who knows?

If you put a headline or message on the outside of the envelope, you run the risk of people dismissing the letter before even opening it. For example, if you received a letter that said, "Inside . . . your chance to buy a new Falcon," you'd be able to instantly decide whether you needed to read the letter or not. And that's before you've seen the pictures or read about the great deals.

Of course, there are effective ways to go about it. What about a letter to business owners that says, "Here's how to get better accountancy advice and pay *no* accountant fees" on the outside. They'd probably have a look.

Always Follow Up with a Phone Call

People generally don't call right after getting a letter; that's just the nature of the game.

However, if you mail them a letter then call soon after, you'll be surprised by the leap in response. People have the chance to ask you questions, and then order directly.

Step 6: When to Mail Your Letters

If your product is perennial (that is, not seasonal), you don't have to be too concerned about when to mail your letter. It's more a question of which day, rather than which time of year.

With business clients, it's usually a good idea to mail them a letter on Tuesday or Wednesday. People are usually feeling too busy on Monday, and pretty uninterested in thinking about anything new on Friday.

If your business is seasonal, you need to approach direct mail differently. For example, a swimming pool builder would find it fruitless mailing a "summer letter" in winter. The business owner would need to adapt the appeal to suit the time of year.

Step 7: What Else Do You Need to Think About?

Use this section as a final checklist. Once you're happy with your direct mail letter, run through and make sure you're ready to get started. Here are a few things you may not have thought of:

Team Training: Do your team members fully understand the strategy you've implemented? It's important they understand the vital role they are to play. If your new customers come in and find the service to be anything but the best, your direct mail campaign will fail.

Objects: Have you included an item with each letter? Check and make sure all letters contain the object you've mentioned in the opening paragraph. Your letter will not make much sense without it.

Check Stock and Team Levels: It's unlikely your direct mail campaign will bring in hundreds of people all at once (very few actually do), but you need to be prepared for a sizable response. There would be nothing worse than having a rush of new customers come in, only to find you have no stock or are too busy to serve them. Plan for your direct mail campaign by making sure you can cater to any increased demand.

"OK, Charlie, so there you have it. That should get you thinking."

"It sure has, Brad. And I've a great idea for my next direct mail campaign. I'm going to keep mine simple to begin with—I can always get more fancy later on. What do you think of this?"

He began writing furiously as if there were no tomorrow, then slid the notepad over to me.

It pays to fire on all cylinders ...

Dear (name),

I've included an old spark plug to make a point—old spark plugs affect the performance of your car.

Let me explain. Most people think they're being conscientious when they send their cars in for a regular minor service. But its not enough to just change the oil and the oil filter. In the past, you've had to 1) be satisfied with just ensuring your car's vital fluids like oil and water were in tip-top condition, 2) spend much more on having a major service done, and 3) do nothing and hope your car continues to perform until you can afford the major service.

Now there's a better way—imagine if you could just have your spark plugs changed.

You could then continue to do your own oil and filter changes, secure in the knowledge that your car's electrical system will also be performing at its best.

I'll phone you in the next couple of days to discuss the idea further. I look forward to speaking with you then.

Charlie

Charlie's Garage

P.S. And of course, we offer a guarantee—if you're not entirely happy with our workmanship or service, we'll give you a complete refund—and your next service *free*.

Example

This time I'm going to give you an example of a successful direct mail letter, only it will be in the form of a template. This is where you get to fill in the relevant pieces of information. You'll soon get the feel of it.

Template of a successful direct mail letter:

Big Headline Expressing Main Benefit and Invoking Curiosity

Dear [name],

I've included a [implement] to make a point. [explanation of why you've included the implement].

Let me explain. [a little more explanation of what you mean, plus more body about the problem]. Here are the 4 main benefits of [doing whatever you're asking the reader to do].

1) **Benefit 1... explanation**

2) **Benefit 2... explanation**

3) **Benefit 3... explanation**

4) **Benefit 4... offer**

[Summing up statement, also tackling any immediate objections, such as and before you say 'I can't afford it,' check this out'].

I'll phone you in the next couple of days to discuss the idea further. I look forward to speaking with you then.

Your name
Position, Your business name

P.S. [Something to sweeten the deal, plus an indication of when the offer ends—make it soon, so they have to take action quickly].

Part 3

▋ Brochures

"Charlie, by the end of this session, you should know exactly how to put together powerful brochures that'll make your prospect want to take *Action*. More importantly, you'll have a selection of new brochures to start testing."

I pushed aside my now-empty coffee mug, dusted off a few crumbs that were the only remaining evidence of a delicious muffin, then continued.

"You'll discover that putting together a great brochure doesn't take great writing skills, nor does it require any knowledge of graphic design. With a little bit of common sense and the information I'm about to give you, you'll be able to create a killer brochure in no time, and it will *work*."

Charlie listened intently as I spoke.

"Our aim isn't to make brochures that look pretty and artistic—the type of brochures you'll create will *sell* for you. In my seminars, I've often advised people to burn their brochures altogether. I have actually demanded that one of the clients I was coaching directly get rid of all of his brochures. And I had good reason. You see, most business owners and salespeople use brochures as a way *not* to sell. Instead of doing the hard work and trying to close the sale on the spot, they just say, "Here, take one of our brochures," and expect the customer to come back. As you'd know yourself, most customers never come back. They keep shopping around until someone gets motivated enough to actually sell them something."

Charlie was nodding as I spoke. I knew he could relate to what I was saying.

"Often, this motivation comes from knowing that the face-to-face sale is the final contact—there are no brochures to fall back on. If the customers walk out, they're gone for good.

Handing out a brochure is really a way of saying, "I'm not sure how to win your business, but if I give you this, I can feel like I've tried my best, and that there is still a chance you'll buy." In circumstances like this, brochures *should* be burned."

I was on a roll now and pressed on, not wanting to lose my train of thought.

"Having said that, a brochure can work as a powerful sales tool when it's used the right way. The trick is knowing how to construct your brochures so they actually encourage someone to *buy*. And this is what I'm going to show you."

"I suppose brochures have a lot in common with newsletters, Brad?"

"Yes, much of what we've discussed will apply. And I'll go over it again. I don't believe in doing anything in half measures. So, to get started, it's back to basics."

What Is a Successful Brochure?

I'm afraid you won't find answers to any great philosophical questions in this book. But more to the point, this section of the book assists you in knowing when you have designed a brochure that really works, and when you haven't.

If you aren't sure what you're aiming for, it's difficult to achieve it. Before even getting started, it's a good idea to consider what's possible, and have an understanding of what isn't. Once you do, you then have a framework to work with. For example: OK, we'd like 1 in every 10 people we give brochures to, to become regular customers.

Before I go any further, answer this: How many brochures have you been given in your life? 20? 100? 300?

For most people, the answer would run into the hundreds. The tendency for salespeople to give out brochures to basically anyone who seems even mildly interested is very common.

As I mentioned before, handing out a brochure is often a substitute for making a sale. They think, "I couldn't be bothered closing this sale, so I'll just hand out a brochure so I can rest easy. At least I've done something."

This kind of thinking is precisely the same as letting a customers walk out when they say, "I want to think about it. I'll get back to you." Come on! How many of these customers ever come back? I'd be amazed if the ratio was any higher than 1 in 20.

By the same token, brochures are also very valuable tools. A good brochure will be retained, and will continue to work as a mobile, colorful ad for your business for maybe months to come.

There are two important things to consider:

First, is there anything about your brochure that gives the customer a reason to hang onto it? Is it anything more than just a picture of your product, some technical specs, and your contact details?

If this is all your brochure contains, you may as well just hand the customer a business card and a picture. In this case, if the customer wants to contact you again, she'll hang onto it. If she's not sure, she will probably throw it away.

A brochure should achieve much more than this!

Second, does your brochure actually encourage the customer to call you and buy? Does it actually *sell* for you?

Perhaps you're thinking a brochure is what the customer looks at first, and then you sell. Wrong!! A brochure can do the whole job, so the customer simply calls you up and says, "Yes, I'd like to order."

Your brochure has to be really good, and well worth hanging onto. I mean, you're asking someone to carry around and keep an ad for your business. And considering how uninterested most people are in advertising, that's a very tall order!

So, How Do You Know When Your Brochure Is Working?

You have to ask people where they heard about you. If you keep hearing, "I have one of your brochures," you're getting a fair indication that your brochures are being retained and read.

The other way to know this is by putting a special offer in your brochure that you don't advertise anywhere else. For example, you could have a line in your brochure that says, "The first time you visit, present this brochure for a 25 percent discount."

If you use the offer approach, make an offer that people will want to come in for. Just saying "5 percent discount" or something similarly miniscule is usually not enough to get people excited (unless you sell a really big-ticket item, like new homes).

In the pages that follow, you'll discover how to make your brochure appealing enough to be held onto, and how to make sure it gets referred to every time the customer needs to buy what you sell.

On a purely financial level, it's worth considering how much you're spending on your brochures, and how much you expect to see back in actual sales.

Brochures are no different than any other marketing tool. You have only so much to spend on marketing and you have to decide where to spend it. If brochures are less cost-effective than newspaper advertising, you may be smarter diverting the funds to the newspaper, rather than the printer. See, if you're given the choice between an investment that gives you a 30 percent return on your money, and one that regularly takes a loss of 15 percent, you'd be insane to keep going with the loss-maker. It would be common sense to divert all your funds towards the 30 percent profit generator, and to keep doing that forever.

Having said that, it also pays to remember the idea of lifetime value when considering the cost-effectiveness of your brochures. Lifetime value is the amount customers are worth to you over the course of their lifetimes. If they come back and visit four times a year, and spend $300 each time, their lifetime value will be $1200 multiplied by how many years they keep coming back.

If you have to hand out $1200 worth of brochures to attract this one customer, then it will take you a year before you see a positive return on investment (assuming very high profit margins).

If the customer turns out to be a very loyal one who returns year after year, and refers lots of friends, it's probably been a good business decision to hand out those 10,000 brochures.

Of course, if your brochures only attract one customer for every 10,000 brochures you hand out, you'd probably want to seriously consider redoing them!

The only real way to judge the success of your brochure is by working out the actual figures—how much are you spending and how much are you seeing back?

It's not always easy to judge with brochures, though. Sometimes customers will get one of your brochures and not buy immediately. You may follow them up on the phone a few weeks later, encourage them into the store, and then get their business.

Did the brochure work? It's hard to say. It didn't directly make the sale, but it certainly contributed. Perhaps the customer wouldn't have bought if it were not for reading the brochure.

In the end, you have to take all factors into account and make an educated decision. You should be able to accurately judge whether people are reading your brochures, and whether they are buying as a result.

The Four Steps to Creating a Great Brochure

Step 1: What Do You Want to Say?

The first thing to work on is what you want to use your brochure for, and what you want to promote in it.

A brochure is different than a newspaper ad in that you can include much more information, and a lot more specific detail. You can give people almost the whole story, and take them right through the sales process.

First, you have to decide whether you are going to use your brochure to promote everything you do, or just one thing. This really depends on whether customers usually use more than one service, or if you offer a variety of things yet customers generally only come in for one.

If it's a case of the latter, where people usually only buy one of your services, you're probably best off designing a brochure for each separate thing you do. There's really no point in confusing people with lots of information about other things that they're not interested in anyway. You should give them a brochure wholly dedicated to the product or service that they're considering buying at that time.

If your business is a little more wide-ranging (such as a photocopy and print shop), it's usually best to design a brochure that promotes all your services. Not only do you get to advertise your other services, you'll have more than enough content to fill a whole brochure. If you were to just advertise one service (for example, photocopying), you'd be flat out filling one page!

Of course, producing one brochure as opposed to a multitude is much cheaper and quicker. But that shouldn't be your main reason. If your business is diverse and specializes in a number of quite different areas, you really should take the time to produce a brochure for each.

The beauty is that you can create a template using this book, then use it as the starting point for all your brochures. That way you get a consistent look across them all. This is an advantage, as multiple brochures that all look completely different can be confusing.

Next, you need to decide your main selling point—the content of the brochure. What is it that you want to tell people about your business or product line?

Many business owners won't really know where to start. As a general rule, it pays to work out your strongest selling point, then go from there.

Almost always, your strongest selling point will be your USP. Remember what I said before about Unique Selling Proposition? It's the one thing that is truly different about you, or at least, the one thing you can promote as being different.

This is really important, so I'll go over it again. A successful USP should be:

- Truly unique

- Exciting to your target market

- Something that will get people talking

- Something that can't be easily copied, or if it can be, it will be an obvious rip-off on the part of the offending business

What about your business? When you started, did you begin with a uniqueness, a real point of difference, or did you just start as a "me-too" competitor?

Here's an interesting example and illustration of why a uniqueness is so important. If you were to open up a new grocery store, you'd have to share sales with all other grocery stores in the area. If there's already three stores, and two of them are already struggling, what makes you think you have a better chance? All you've done is split the sales further. Now, instead of the total area grocery sales being split between three, they have to be split between four.

If you start the business as a "me-too," you can forget it. The days of competing on price and service are starting to end. These days, people have so many options they can almost always get it somewhere cheaper, from someone who'll do it better.

The major point is clear—you must *stand out*. If you have no uniqueness, you have no reason for existence. Remember, as new competitors come into the market, you'll continue to sink. If there's no reason for customers to continue coming to you, and not them, you'll keep losing business. It's a gloomy forecast, but a realistic one.

You must work out your uniqueness, and you must do it *now*.

So how do you go about it? And what do you do if you don't really have *anything* that makes you unique at all? By the way, it's pretty common to find businesses that are exactly the same as a dozen others and within close range. For a prime example, think about almost any Chinese restaurant you've ever been to.

For a start, list everything you do that could be considered even a little bit unique. These points don't have to be earth shattering—just different enough to matter. To get your mind started, here is a list of some possible USPs you could adopt:

- You sell a higher-quality product or service, and you can specifically show how it benefits the customer in a meaningful way.

- You provide more/better customer service, and you can easily explain and promote why you're better.

- You offer a better/longer guarantee, and you have it written down.

- You offer more choice/selection/options, and this is something that people want and always look for.

- You offer a trade-in program, and no one else does.

- You serve a specific (yet sizable) demographic group that is overlooked by most competitors.

- You offer a better/more generous bonus points or loyalty club system, and your product or service is at least as good.

- You offer better overall value for money.

- You have the best after-sales service, and this is something you can easily explain to people when they buy.

- Your product or service has unique features that people care about.

- You have supercheap products and services that cater to people who want the most basic thing available.

- You have ultraexpensive products and services that cater to those who only want the best and will pay anything to have it.

- You deal only with a set number of customers, and only those of a particular type.

- You offer attractive products or services that no one else does.

- You have a "special ingredient."

- You install and deliver for free.

- You bring the goods to the customers and let them choose in their own homes.

- You send a video catalog, take the order over the phone, and deliver within a set time period.

- You have a "one-price" approach—everything in your store is one price, regardless of what it is.

- You run an ongoing competition, such as every 13th customer wins $50.

- The atmosphere of your store is completely unlike anything else, either in terms of its tranquility or activity.

- Your staff are all of a certain type, age group, background, or experience level.

- You are the fastest and guarantee to finish the job much more quickly than anyone else.

Surely, from this list you can find something you are currently doing that is unique. Perhaps it is possible that you'll discover something you *should* be doing that would make you unique.

Basically, your uniqueness comes from one of seven areas: quality, price, service, delivery, speed, convenience, and experience.

In case you're wondering, "experience" means the actual experience of buying from you. Imagine a video store that has four 11-foot-wide screens that constantly play the latest releases all day and night. That would be a real experience.

Once you've decided what your uniqueness is, it's time to write it down. This is important because it will soon be communicated to your team and your customers.

It needs to be summed up by a one- or two-line statement. Think, "Always Coca Cola," or "Toyota: Oh, What a Feeling." Of course, your USP doesn't have to be something that sounds like it came straight from the brain of a pony-tailed advertising person. It'll probably work twice as well if it doesn't.

There's nothing wrong with this USP: "Jim's Video—the only video store in Wollongong with four 11-foot screens playing the latest releases."

Just state your uniqueness plainly and simply. How about "Marie's hairdressing—where colors, streaks, and perms are half the price and twice the quality," or "Sally's industrial safety equipment—456 different items always in stock, and free delivery."

It's great to be specific. If you can put a number in your USP, that's ideal. Think about the "11 herbs and spices," or the "32 flavors." These are USPs that stick in your mind. A beautician could say, 'Beauty Shop: 4 qualified and friendly beauticians with more than 23 years of experience each."

Now its time to write yours. Don't worry too much about the wording; just get the point across. If you show it to people and they don't seem to understand, you may want to rethink it. If they seem to get the idea immediately, you're on the right track.

Once you've determined your USP, it's not a bad idea to make this the focus of your brochure. This is the *main* reason people should deal with you and not somebody else. Remember, your USP needs to be strong. You can't just say, "Harry's Hardware—where the service is good." People won't have any reaction to that, and anyone can claim it anyway.

On the other hand, *not* everyone can claim their entire team of employees used to be tradespeople. The important thing is, customers of a hardware store would probably care about this type of thing, and the USP would give them a reason to shop at Harry's and *not* somewhere else.

Remember, if you are a hardware store owner offering "good service" as your USP, and there is another hardware store offering "good service" as theirs, customers have no reason to shop at one place in preference to the other.

Once you've determined your USP, then it's a good idea to create the supporting points. Apart from your USP, what else do you do well?

To get your mind rolling, try filling in the blanks here:

Seven reasons why customers should deal with me and not someone else.

1. _____
2. _____
3. _____
4. _____
5. _____
6. _____
7. _____

How did you do? Did you come up with seven good reasons? If not, think harder. This exercise will reveal more about your business than anything you've done for a long time. The fact is, if you can't think of seven reasons why people should come to you and not to your competitors, you should go back and reread the section on USPs.

Of course, sometimes the question isn't really about your competitors. Perhaps you're doing a brochure for a product that is truly unique to begin with. Perhaps you're really wondering whether people will buy it.

Instead of choosing between you and your competition, they are deciding between whether to buy or not to buy. They don't *need* what you are selling, but if you convince them, they'll purchase.

If that's the case for you, you need to work out the seven reasons people should buy your product or service. Once you have your seven reasons, it's time to put them in order. What are the most important selling points? You don't have unlimited space, so you may need to omit some of the points altogether.

Next, it's time to write your text.

The main thing to remember about writing a brochure is that you're not writing one continuous stream of prose. While you might have a start and end with a newspaper ad, a brochure is usually broken up into three or four different sections. For example, a car brochure might have one section headlined "Performance to burn (up the road)," another section entitled "Stylish inside and out," and a final section called "And your servicing is booked for the first two years."

You can imagine the writers of that brochure going through the "seven-reasons" approach. They probably decided the three most important points worth considering were performance, style, and scheduled service. Once they'd come up with the subjects, they then wrote a little piece on each, probably of about 50–100 words each.

You can imagine how they put the rest together. After writing the text, they came up with headlines for each minisection. Then, they made a front cover, which would probably be the picture of the car and a headline like "The most luxurious car ever released for under $28,000." Last, they'd add in the dealer's contact details, and supporting pictures.

That's all fine and dandy, and a good start, but the aim should be to approach things a little differently.

So How Do You Go About That?

First, you should make every subheadline strong. Instead of "performance to burn," the writers of the above brochure could have written something like "Four ways you'll know this car performs better than any you've ever driven."

From there, it really writes itself. The "stylish inside and out" could have been "we've put in all the usual things, plus 11 modern conveniences you won't find on any other car." The last section could have been titled "Amazing . . . $780 worth of servicing—free." These headlines are much more specific and grabbing.

In addition to the improved subheadlines, the front cover could have had the headline "If you're planning to buy a new car, here are three reasons why you'll soon be driving a Maxima." Alternately, they could have gone with something like "So you're buying a new car?" or "Stop!! Don't buy a new car before reading this."

At this point, you may be thinking: "That's great, but I don't know how to write headlines like that."

Problem solved—you'll find a quick tutorial in Part 6 of this book.

Remember, you need to pull out every "gun" you have in your arsenal on your brochure. First, hit readers with your USP up front, then break it up into three or four main points, each with powerful subheads, then close the deal with a strong offer to get them to act.

Don't stop rewriting the text of your brochure until you're thinking: "Yeah, we are the best, and we're offering the best deal anyone will find in this town." If you believe it, it's likely your customers will too.

It pays to keep in mind that your customers aren't that different than you. I can hear some business owners choking when they read this! They're people, and they won't get motivated unless you really motivate them.

You always have to ask yourself this when writing a brochure or a headline— so what? If you write down "we've been in business for three years," ask yourself "so what?" and then think of another way to put it. What about "unlike so many of our competitors, we've been here for three years," meaning "we'll be here if there's ever a problem—and that means after-sales service."

You could ask yourself "so what?" again, then approach it from a different angle: "Our after-sales service means you'll never be without your [product] for more than 24 hours. We've been in business three years and will be here to help with anything long after our 'backyard' competitors have gone bust."

Keep rewriting until you're absolutely convinced by your own words. See, many people think they can't write. The problem is they expect to get it right the first time. Even the best writers have to rewrite things over and over again.

Since this is the only time you'll have to write this brochure, why not take the time to make it the very best it can be? You may amaze yourself; when you keep improving your original effort, your text will get better and better. Keep in mind that people reading your brochure will be indifferent; they don't care about you or what you're offering. You have to win them over.

Tell them everything they want to hear, and then tell it to them again.

Finally, you should consider including a guarantee. A successful and powerful guarantee should be:

- Specific

- Something that addresses the main frustrations and fears of the customer when dealing with your industry

- Be complete—it should say "either this happens or we'll do this"

- Impressive

People have been burned before. They've used products they were told were fantastic, only to be bitterly disappointed. You must take that risk away for them.

To understand how and why, you need to understand this—when customers buy, they are not buying your product or service. They are buying the benefit of owning or experiencing whatever it is you sell. For example, people don't buy lawn mowers; they are buying a lawn that is properly mowed and the feeling of being house-proud that comes with it. Here's another example: Customers don't buy food; they buy satisfaction, survival, and the pleasure of eating. In the case of a restaurant, they are also buying an experience and a social occasion.

If you guarantee to give people the benefits they are after in the first place, there is a high chance they'll want to deal with you. Imagine a hairdresser who had a special guarantee for every single person who had her haircut on a Saturday morning. The guarantee reads like this: "If you don't look the best you ever have on Saturday night and get three times as much interest from the opposite sex, we will pay for you to see another hairdresser."

Remember, people aren't buying a haircut—they are buying a look and the feeling of looking their best. You could go really deep with the psychology of that one—people want to look their best because they want acceptance. They want acceptance because they want to feel good about themselves. They want to feel good about themselves because they want to feel as though they are worthwhile people, which is one of the most basic human needs.

Phew! I bet you thought you were just cutting their hair. It's important to keep in mind you are selling more than just the product. If people are unsure that they will get the main benefit from dealing with you, they may hesitate when it comes to actually buying, or they may buy from someone else who makes them feel more secure.

It's all about understanding what makes the customers tick, then absolutely guaranteeing to give them that. If they don't feel they have received what you promised, they get compensation.

When people feel as though they have "nothing to lose," they are more likely to buy and take action. Most action is delayed forever, simply because people are afraid of what will happen if they make a mistake. Imagine if every customer who came to you thought: "Well, I can't lose with these guys. I'll buy it now and see how it works out."

A guarantee can shoot you ahead in the sale process too. If people already feel certain that they will get what they set out to get, they will be less worried about spending time obsessing over every detail.

If there's ever a problem, they know they can come back and get their money back. Of course, you need to make sure the product you are recommending is the right one for their needs. And naturally, if your product or service isn't up to snuff, a guarantee may kill your business. However, if 98 percent of your customers are happy, and you are satisfied with your product or service, then guarantee away. If people always seem to be happy, why not guarantee that they will be?

Many business owners are frightened of guarantees. They honestly think customers will rip them off.

The truth is this that most guarantees are never taken advantage of, even when the customer is genuinely dissatisfied. There are two reasons why. First, people are lazy, and can't be bothered. Second, it takes a lot of confidence to stand up and say: "Hey, I'm not happy. Give me my money back." The fact is, most people lack that sort of confidence. That's not to say that there aren't people out there who will rip you off. You'll get the occasional pathetic person who buys an item, uses it a couple of times, then returns it for no other reason than that it's already served its purpose. These people know they are doing the wrong thing and have a sense of guilt. If you prick that guilt, they'll usually go away. When they phone to tell you they want to return something, ask some very direct questions like:

- "So what is it you don't like about the item?"
- "How many times have you used it?"
- "So what are you going to buy instead?"

Make sure the people are returning the items so they can buy something else. Your guarantee should not cater to people who buy things they don't need and can't afford.

If you ask these questions, many of these sleazy people will back off. There's nothing wrong with making them work for their refund either. Why not get them to fill out a three-page feedback form explaining what the problems were along with all their personal details. Encourage them to take it away, and fill it out at home.

The people with genuine problems with the item will come back with the form; the rest will see it as too hard.

Of course, these customers are the last thing to worry about. Your new powerful guarantee will bring you more customers overall, so it's worth taking that small chance.

So, What Should You Guarantee, and How Should You Write It?

The best way is to completely forget about what you can do. Let's rather think about what your customers want. Once you know what they want, let's work out how you can promise to give it to them.

OK, to begin with, let's work out the biggest frustration customers have when dealing with you.

If it's builders dealing with subcontractors, it's almost always people not showing up. If it's people getting their haircut, it's usually the hairdresser's taking too much off and making them look silly. If it's a gym, it's often they feel uncomfortable letting their blubber fly in front of a bunch of tanned, well-toned Greek gods and gym bunnies.

Think about it—what really bugs your customers? Get into their shoes, then consider saying, "If I could just find a [business type] that did [x], I'd deal with him every time and recommend all my friends too."

OK, now fill in the blanks. What is that one thing? Got it? Now how can you guarantee to do that for them? Don't immediately rule out the possibility—there are dentists out there that guarantee no pain, no waiting, and no surprises. There are pest control companies that guarantee you won't *see* a bug for six months, there are hairdressers who guarantee to fit a hair extension free if they chop off too much, and there are video stores that let you watch another video free if you don't like the movie.

The impossible can be achieved. Of course, that one thing may be achievable and you may have to ask yourself whether it's economically viable.

OK, if you can't do the first one, let's move on to the next biggest frustration.

Think about it—what else bugs your customers?

Now let's develop a guarantee based on that. Can't be done? Move onto the next one, but make sure you're giving each one a fair chance of success. If you're just avoiding a killer guarantee for fear of doing more work or having to rearrange the business, you're cheating yourself.

Once you know what you want to guarantee, it's time to write it down. This will be promoted on all of your business cards and your letterhead, so it pays to take the time with it.

The basic format for a powerful guarantee is simple: "If this doesn't happen, then we'll do that." For example, "If your friends don't start commenting on your immaculately clear skin within four weeks, you get every dollar back and a voucher for a free consultation with a dermatologist (value $80)." How much business is that guarantee going to get a beautician?

OK, let's write yours.

First, write the first part of your guarantee. This is where you promise something will happen. It's good idea to phrase it along these lines: "If you're not blah blah blah," or "You will blah blah blah," with the next words being "If not, we'll blah blah blah." Make the actual promise as specific as you can. Put a time frame on it and make it really stand out.

Explain what will happen. This is the real benefit of buying the product or service.

Second, write the "this-will-happen" bit—don't be afraid of "money back," or a "we'll keep working with you until you get the results" guarantee.

Another option is, "We'll pay for you to see our most hated competitor," or "We'll write you a check for the amount you invested plus $1000 to go to your favorite charity." Now that's powerful!! Of course, it depends on the industry.

Here's a simple guarantee. All you need to do now is fill in the blanks.

"I personally guarantee you will [promise]. If not, we will [what will happen]."

OK, let's summarize what you need to write:

- It's important to come up with a USP. This is the main thing that sets you apart from your competitors, and the most important reason people should deal with you. This should be the main thrust of your brochure and the basis of your main headline.

- You need to work the three or four most important selling benefits. Write a little section for each, and come up with a subheadline strong enough to get people reading each section. Use the headline starters in this section to get the ball rolling.

- Come up with an offer that will encourage people to act, and soon. This offer should give you the edge over the competition.

- It's a good idea to print your business guarantee somewhere on the brochure, usually near the end. The reasoning is simple—you get people a fair way down the sales path then hit them with the guarantee. You want them to think "Wow, they do x, y, and z, they're giving away a, b and c and they have this guarantee too—I can't lose!"

- Last, you'll need a section with your contact details. This should be easy enough. One recommendation worth noting: Include a "where-to-find-us map" next to your details. People prefer these to just an address. One last thing: Make your phone number big. For some reason, a bigger phone number seems to encourage people to call.

Step 2: How Do You Want Your Brochure to Look?

When it comes to designing your brochure, forget about art and abstract nonsense. Just put it right out of your mind, because it will only lead you down the garden path. I remember dealing with a client who decided to make a horse the focus of her logo and brochure. So she used a picture of a horse on the front cover.

Her business was corporate sales training. When I asked her why she chose a horse as her main image, she said: "Horses have always been a big part of my life, and I wanted a logo that gets that across."

I found it hard to keep a straight face.

Obviously, she is the only person that cares about her interest in horses—the corporations that are considering contracting her services for sales training don't give a damn. The cutesy horse picture was more confusing than anything else, and did nothing to add to the appeal of her business. She had plenty of justification for the logo: She believed horses were swift and noble—exactly the qualities she could teach salespeople. It all sounded like rubbish to me, and just a convenient explanation of her choice to put a horse on her business cards. If she'd just said, "I like horses" and left it at that, I'd probably have more respect for the idea. It's her business, after all.

I think people have a real inbuilt "trash" detector, and we find it difficult to swallow all of this artsy nonsense. If it sells, it sells. If it looks good, it looks good. There really isn't anything else to it.

Having said that, it's important to note that different colors, images, and fonts give people different impressions. Subconsciously, we associate different looks with different ideas. For example, if you used an old Gothic typeface, people would think of you as classic, steeped in tradition, and maybe British in heritage.

If you used a computer-style typeface, people might see you as modern and up-to-date. If you used a handwritten, or comic typeface, people would be more inclined to view you as informal and fun.

The thing is, you don't need any special education to work this stuff out—you already know it. If an image suggests something to you, it's very likely it will suggest the same thing to most other people too. That doesn't include things like horses, which mean very different things to different people.

When designing your brochure, the key is to think about every aspect in terms of *sales*. Whenever you're deciding whether to include a picture, diagram, or design, you should be asking yourself, "Will it add to the chances of someone's buying my product or service?"

Often, business owners just throw in whatever pictures they have, or whatever drawings wholesalers have given them. They use these things to fill up space. Ultimately, this approach is virtually useless. Why go to the trouble and expense of producing a new brochure if you're not going to go all the way?

Everything should have a reason for being there, and that means every word and every picture. If you need to go out and get some more pictures done, then go and do it. Don't skimp! A brochure is usually a one-time affair, so it's best to get it right from the outset. Besides, once you have your text written, it should be pretty obvious what you need to do: The size, the pictures, the typeface, and so on.

Let's deal with each aspect of the brochure's "look," one at a time.

Typefaces

As mentioned earlier, there are two basic types, sans serif and serif. The most common type of serif font is Times New Roman. The most common sans serif font is called Arial. Times gives a more classic feel, while Arial seems more modern.

Computers offer a huge range of fonts, and it's cheap and easy to lay your hands on some more. You may end up with too wide a choice, which will ultimately slow you down. It's best to choose a basic font that looks good, and that suits your image. Try and use a serif font for the main body text. Your printer or graphic designer will almost certainly recommend Arial or Helvetica (both are sans serif fonts). To their artistic eyes, Times New Roman just looks plain. Don't worry about that. The fonts you use in your headlines will give your brochure its character. The font you use for your main text just needs to be easy to read.

Pictures and Drawings

Brochures are one medium where pictures are just as important as the words. People like to "look through" brochures; they don't necessarily want to read them. Your brochure needs to have enough visual content to be satisfying to them, before they read the text. By that I mean the pictures have to tell a large part of the story themselves.

Think about car brochures. Many people never even read the text; they just look at the pictures.

See, many of us don't make decisions in a particularly logical way. We may pretend we do by making up reasons and justifications, but in the end, we are generally led by our emotions. Pictures can stir up an emotion much easier than text can. It's the difference between hearing about something and being there. People don't want to be told about a new car; they want to see it!

In general, a picture will work much better than a drawing will. In the case of a diagram, the opposite is true. Line art works well.

There are also other visual elements you should consider: Tables of facts work particularly well, comparison charts are always looked at (where you compare the specifications of your product and those of your competitors), and a picture of yourself (the business owner) with a personal statement underneath is often a great credibility builder.

Of course, much of this depends on how much space you have. I'd recommend trimming the text if you have a really good picture that needs more room. Remember, everything you put in must sell. If your words sell more than the picture you're thinking about, keep the text. If the pictures tell more than the story, cut the words.

Avoid squashing the text into really small type—anything under 9-point type is getting hard to read.

Color

The same considerations apply here as with newsletters. But remember, your photos should show the product in "real life," and color is the only way to achieve this. If you're going to use color, it's worth noting the impact of color psychology:

- Forest Green—appeals to the wealthy but may cause rejection in other economic groups

- Burgundy—same as forest green

- Bluish Red—appeals to women

- Yellowish Red—appeals to men

- Orange—makes people think the business is informal and open to everyone

- Yellow—gets attention, but can indicate cheapness

- White—good color for decor, and reminds people of dairy products and cleanliness

Ultimately, I recommend you trust your own instincts before worrying about the rules. Your opinion is just as valid as anybody else's—we've all grown up in the same society, and all have basically the same understanding of what colors mean. For example, light blue will always be associated with clear skies. Red always means stop; green generally means go, or nature.

Start paying attention to other brochures, and see if you can work out why they've chosen the colors they have. Also, note the impact that the colors have on your opinion of the business.

One strong recommendation: Keep it simple! Putting too many colors in will only make your brochure look like a technicolor nightmare. The fewer colors, the better. Limit yourself to about three (not including the photos, which will be full color), and then tastefully apply them to your brochure.

Layout

Many people fall into the trap of trying to jazz up their brochures by throwing in lots of different shapes and elements. Unless you have a good deal of artistic ability, you're best sticking with a simple layout.

Basically, you should aim to have one picture on each panel, and one block of text. Often, you will have one panel that is completely devoted to a picture of the product. It all depends on how many elements you have to squeeze in and what size your brochure is. This is covered in the next section.

The thing to remember is this: It's all very straightforward. You don't need anything more than common sense to put together a brochure. If it looks too cluttered, take some things out. If it looks too barren, add more in. If it looks like there's too much text, add some more pictures.

The easiest way to get your layout right is to use the templates included at the end of this section, or to copy another brochure that you like.

If you want to try something out of the ordinary, you should pay a graphic designer to do it for you. Professional designers can be quite expensive. If you want to save some money, remember about the college or university option. Graphic design students are usually eager to get work experience, and earn some money at the same time.

Size

Most brochures are either normal letter size or three-fold size (known as A4 and DL outside North America). Three-fold is generally the best option. Not only is it the most widely used and accepted, it's also the easiest and cheapest to produce. It will fit into brochure holders that you can buy from stores that sell shop fittings.

Really, you should only consider another format if you have a large amount of information that *must* be included, or if the product/service you're selling is a really big-ticket item. For example, I'd expect more than a DL brochure if I were considering buying a new Porsche. I'd want a full-color, 20-page extravaganza. The same goes for new homes.

You may wish to try an odd-sized or shaped card. This can certainly make your brochure stand out, but again, unless you have great artistic flair, you're best advised to consult a professional designer, printer, or a member of the *Action International* creative team.

Stock

Stock is the term used for the type of paper or card you print your brochure on. There are numerous types from which to choose. Should you use glossy paper or plain paper? Plain card or a textured card? Normal weight or something a little heavier? These are just some of the questions to be answered when choosing your stock.

Just as there are a variety of materials available, there are also a variety of prices, going from the very expensive to the downright cheap. Before deciding on the type you want to use for your brochure, you need to consider the type of product you're about to promote.

If you're selling expensive, good-quality products, it's better to use good-quality stock. For a cheap, consumable product or service, cheaper stock is fine. People generally aren't that concerned, but they may find it strange if your high-quality business promotes itself using the cheapest and thinnest stock available.

Step 3: Where Should You Get Them Printed?

Once you've designed your brochure, and decided on the stock, you then have to decide where and how to get it printed. This will depend largely on your budget. You basically have three choices:

- Professional printer: This is more expensive but ensures your brochure will look first-rate. Always have your brochure professionally printed if your budget allows.

- Personal printer: If you own, or have access to, a good-quality computer laser printer, you may be able to save on your printing cost. However, you need to keep in mind the quality of the stock you use. If you were printing a large number of brochures, it would probably be more cost-effective in the long run to have them done professionally. Printing 1000 color brochures on your own printer will probably be impractical anyway.

- Photocopies: From a cost point of view, this is the bargain basement of printing. If you decide to go with this option, make sure the quality of reproduction is high. Most instant print businesses produce remarkably good jobs these days. An added benefit of opting for this route is that they will do all the necessary collating, folding, stitching, and packaging as well. But beware of the cheap do-it-yourself option. Having black "photocopier lines" all over your brochure will make you, and your product, look cheap. Only use this option as a last resort, and only for black-and-white jobs. Color photocopying will always work out to be too expensive to really consider.

Step 4: How Should You Use Them?

Once you have your brochures together, it's time to get them out there. Let's look at the different ways you can use them:

- As a sales generator: If your brochure is self-contained (it tells the whole story), you can use it as a flyer. This works best when you have a list of qualified prospects, and you can send it directly to them, addressed with their name. The other option is a PO box drop.

- As a sales tool: The best way to incorporate brochures into your sales process is to take the customers through it yourself. Sit down with them, and explain the different aspects of your product or service, using your brochure as a common reference point. You can point out information and pictures using the brochure. If you don't close the sale then and there, the customer can take the brochure away.

- As a presales tool: Often, people just want information. They are planning to buy, but they want to sit down and have a look at some brochures first. This is when it's fine to just send a brochure out, although I'd recommend that you get the customers' details and then follow up on the phone after they've had it for a few days.

- As a referral tool: If your brochure is interesting and appealing, you can give multiple copies to various customers, so they can hand them on to friends.

"What do you think, Charlie?" I continued after a slight pause. I was concerned he was experiencing information overload.

"I'm doing fine, Brad. It just staggers me that this is all new to me. I mean, here I am running a successful business and yet I know so little about business. I feel I must have been succeeding despite my best efforts, if you know what I mean."

"Yes, I do, Charlie, and you're not alone. Most small business owners are in the same boat. And that's what I'm setting out to correct. Understand how much more successful you will become by making a few small changes to the way you think and act. Imagine how your business will grow and prosper when you begin applying some of these instant tools. And remember, the more you do it, the better you'll become at it. The more you test and measure, the more effective your marketing strategies will become. It's not rocket science, you know."

"That's what's blowing me away, Brad. I keep thinking to myself, I can do this!"

"I'm glad you've realized that. Here, have a look at these simple examples. They'll help you when the time comes to think about designing a brochure of your own."

Examples

Here are some examples for you to consider. You can use them as a guide to design your own brochures.

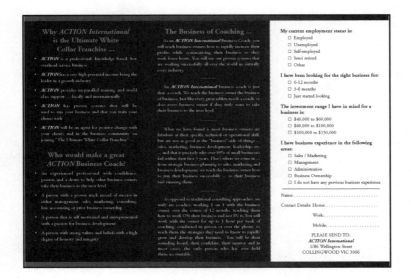

Template of a successful brochure

Special Offer Goes Here

Dot-pointed Service List Goes Here ...

Lorem et iusto odio dignissim qui blandit praesent luptatum zzril delenit au gue duis dolore te feugat nulla facilisi. Ut wisi enim ad orpersuscipit lobortis nisl ut aliqu ip ex en commodo consequat.

- Service you provide
- Service you provide
- Service you provide
- Service you provide
- Service you provide
- Service you provide
- Service you provide

Your Headline Goes Here

Sub-heading Goes Here ...

Lorem et iusto odio dignissim qui blandit praesent luptatum zzril delenit au gue duis dolore te feugat nulla facilisi. Ut wisi enim ad orpersuscipit lobortis nisl ut aliqu ip ex en commodo consequat.

- Benefit
- Benefit
- Benefit
- Benefit
- Benefit
- Benefit
- Benefit

Duis te feugifacilisi.per. yj tyjk tyjkt rth yjetyjt. Jhb rg sfgn lobortis nisl ut aliqu ip ex en commodo dfg db consequat. Duis tbortis nisl ut aliqu ip ex en commodo dfg db consequat. Duis e feugifacilisi.per. yj tyjk dghmdgm. The eh tyj fsbn yj tyuk gfjmyu.

Lorem et iusto odio dignissim qui blandit praesent luptatum zzril delemm. yj tyjk tyjkt rth yjetyjt. Jhb rg sfgn lobortis nisl ut yj tyjk dghmdgm. The eh tyj fsbn yj tyuk gfjmyu.

Photo Goes Here

Your Logo

Your Logo

Contact Details Go Here
Phone Fax
Address

Sub-Heading

Your Main Headline Goes Here ...

Lorem et iusto odio dignissim qui blandit praesent luptatum zzril delenit au gue duis dolore te feugat nulla facilisi. Ut wisi enim ad orpersuscipit lobortis nisl ut aliqu ip ex en commodo consequat.

Duis te feugifacilisi.per. yj tyjk tyjkt rth yjetyjt. Jhb rg sfgn lobortis nisl ut aliqu ip ex en commodo dfg db consequat. Duis tbortis nisl ut aliqu ip ex en commodo dfg db consequat. Duis e feugifacilisi.per. yj tyjk dghmdgm. The eh tyj fsbn yj tyuk gfjmyu.

Lorem et iusto odio dignissim qui blandit praesent luptatum zzril delenit au gue duis dolore te feugat nulla facilisi. Ut wisi enim ad orpersuscipit lobortis nisl ut aliqu ip ex en commodo consequat.

Duis te feugifacilisi.per. yj tyjk tyjkt rth yjetyjt. Jhb rg sfgn lobortis nisl ut aliqu ip ex en commodo dfg db consequat. Duis tbortis nisl ut aliqu ip ex en commodo dfg db consequat. Duis e feugifacilisi.per. yj tyjk dghmdgm. The eh tyj fsbn yj tyuk gfjmyu.

Lorem et iusto odio dignissim qui blandit praesent luptatum zzril delemm. yj tyjk tyjkt rth yjetyjt. Jhb rg sfgn lobortis nisl ut yj tyjk dghmdgm. The eh tyj fsbn yj tyuk gfjmyu.

Lorem et iusto odio dignissim qui blandit praesent luptatum zzril deleLorem et iusto odio dignissim qui blandit praesent luptatum zzrorpersuscipit lobortis nsequat. nit au gue duis dolore te feugat nulla facilisi. Ut wisi enim ad orpersuscipit lobortis nisl ut aliqu ip ex en commodo consequat.

Photo

Photo

Sub-heading Goes Here ...

Lorem et iusto odio dignissim qui blandit praesent luptatum zzril dedelenit au gue duis dolore te feugat nulla facilisi. Ut wisi edelenit au gue duis dolore te feugat nulla facilisi. Ut edelau gue duis dolore te feugat nulla facilisi. Ut wisi elenit au gue duis dolore lobortis nisl ut aliqu ip ex en commodo consequat.

Duis te feugifacilisi.per. yj tyjk tyjkt rth yjetyjt. Jhb rg sfgn lobortis nisl ut aliqu ip ex en commodo dfg db consequat. Duis e fsi.per. yj tyjk dghmdgm. The eh tyj fsbn yj tyuk gfjmyu.

Sub-heading Goes Here ...

Lorem et iusto odio dignissim qui blandit praesent luptatum zzril delenit au gue duis dolore te feugat nulla facilisi. Ut wisi enim ad orpersuscipit lobortis nisl ut aliqu ip ex en commodo consequat.

Duis te feugifacilisi.per. yj tyjk tyjkt rth yjetyjt. Jhb rg sfgn lobortis nisl ut aliqu ip ex en commodo dfg db consequat. Duis tbortis nisl ut aliqu ip ex en commodo dfg db consequat. Duis e feugifacilisi.per. yj tyjk dghmdgm. The eh tyj fsbn yj tyuk gfjmyu.

Lorem et iusto odio dignissim qui blandit praesent luptatum zzril delenit au gue duis dolore te feugat nulla facilisi. Ut wisi enim ad orpersuscipit lobortis nisl ut aliqu ip ex en commodo consequat.

Duis te feugifacilisi.per. yj tyjk tyjkt rth yjetyjt. Jhb rg sfgn lobortis nisl ut aliqu ip ex en commodo dfg db consequat. Duis tbortis nisl ut aliqu ip ex en commodo dfg db consequat. Duis e feugifacilisi.per. yj tyjk dghmdgm. The eh tyj fsbn yj tyuk gfjmyu.

Lorem et iusto odio dignissim qui blandit praesent luptatum zzril delemm. yj tyjk tyjkt rth yjetyjt. Jhb rg sfgn lobortis nisl ut yj tyjk dghmdgm. The eh tyj fsbn yj tyuk gfjmyu.

$$\boxed{\textbf{Part 4}}$$

■ Flyers

"Charlie, we're now going to have a closer look at flyers and what it takes to produce great ones that work. But before we get into that, I must mention at this point that I love flyers for two reasons: first, they're cheap, effective, and easy to produce. And second, they're a great way to test more elaborate and expensive advertising campaigns."

"What do you mean, Brad?"

"Well, remember when I mentioned how important it is to test and measure everything?"

He nodded.

"Well, if you're thinking of placing large advertisements in the newspaper, for instance, you'd be wasting a lot of money if the ad didn't work. So, to reduce the risk you run, you'd test your headline or offer first, wouldn't you?"

Again he nodded.

"And one of the best ways of doing this in a real-life market situation is with flyers. You see, if you had two or three different concepts you wanted to try, to see which gets the best response, you could simply design a different flyer for each, have it distributed in your target area, and measure the results. The one that scores highest is the one you run with for your newspaper ad. Get it?"

"Yeah, I see what you mean, man. That's brilliant."

"No, just sensible, Charlie. Now if you were to understand the various factors that contribute towards a successful flyer, you'd have no trouble at all writing one up whenever needed. So, lets get straight into it then with a look at the basics."

What Is a Successful Flyer Campaign?

Go to the mailbox of any household on a Saturday morning and it will generally be overflowing with flyers. While average people will read them, very few will ever be acted upon. There have been many examples of companies who send out 40,000 flyers and only get four positive responses.

A successful flyer campaign will, of course, perform much better than this. But even an effective campaign will not generate a 100 percent response rate. A realistic target would be between 15 percent and 25 percent for the average campaign.

Basically, any campaign that pays for itself can be considered successful. But before embarking on a flyer campaign, there are a few things you need to understand.

Work out your costs: This includes the cost of printing, envelopes (if you use them), any implements you put in the envelopes, and obviously the cost of having them delivered.

Know your margins: You need to know the net profit you make from anyone who buys your product or service. By understanding how much you actually make from each sale, you'll be able to work out the percentage response required to make your campaign profitable.

Lifetime value: Don't view each new customer your campaign brings in as a one-time sale. You will normally lose money on the first sale to a new client. Remember, the average business will need to sell to a client two times before it begins to make a profit.

With this in mind, you need to focus on bringing the customer back on a regular basis. Therefore, any campaign that covers its cost initially will turn out to be profitable in the long term.

What Makes a Successful Flyer Campaign?

Understanding that our aim is to achieve a response rate of somewhere between 15 percent and 25 percent, we need to look at the individual components of that campaign. We'll deal with these components one by one in a moment, but first we need to identify them individually.

Targeted area: You don't want to deliver your flyers in an area where nobody would be interested in your product or service.

Headline: This is the most important part of your flyer. If it doesn't grab your reader's attention immediately, your campaign will fail.

Body copy: Once your headline has attracted the reader's attention, you need to convey the benefits of buying your product or services in a clear, believable, and easy-to-read fashion.

Envelope: If you decide to use one, then this is the first thing your prospect will see. If you don't put some thought and effort into designing an effective envelope, chances are it won't be opened and your flyer won't get read.

In the following pages you'll learn how to lay out an effective flyer. You will be shown in easy-to-follow steps how to write effective headlines, how to structure your body copy for maximum impact, and how to position photographs to increase your response rate.

Then you'll discover the types of offers that get the phone running hot and those that don't. I'll give you practical tips on how to "dress your flyers up" to make sure they avoid the trash can. And finally I'll provide you with a number of templates for you to use to create your own successful flyer campaign.

The Seven Steps to Creating Powerful Flyers

Step 1: Why Use Flyers?

Before writing anything, you need to work out whether flyers are the best approach (*or at least, one of the best approaches*) for you. But let's think about it a little more deeply.

You need to think about your product or service; is it instantly appealing and easy to explain? If not, you'll have a hard time getting the message across in a flyer.

Most flyers only get a moment's notice before being firmly chucked in the garbage can. People don't like junk mail, and they feel no guilt tossing the lot with only a cursory glance. If your flyer is going to work, you need to make sure your product or service can be explained in a few words. More importantly, you need something that grabs people's attention—a great offer, a powerful point of difference, or something new.

And you need to be realistic—10 percent off the price of fish and chips is barely going to encourage anybody to act. On the other hand, a package deal with two servings of fish plus two servings of chips for $4.95 might. Even if this is more than people would normally pay, you'll probably still get calls. The reason is simple: The offer and package are easy to understand, and they're attractive.

If you need more explanation and more time to get the message across, maybe flyers aren't the ideal way to go. Flyers work best when you can say everything in about seven words or fewer. For example, "Free Chocolate Éclairs" says enough, and so does "Now available . . . in-home men's haircuts for $5."

Also, it pays to remember that flyers can cheapen your image. Here's an illustration: Imagine you got a brochure in the mail from IBM, or QANTAS. You'd probably think it was a little unusual. Not only that, you might think these businesses were getting a little desperate. On the other hand, there's nothing at all strange about getting a flyer from your local Chinese restaurant or stationery supplier.

Step 2: Who Is Your Target Market?

So you've decided to do a flyer promotion. But to whom are you going to send them? Your target market is an important consideration when sending them out. Mailbox drops can be very costly if you don't get your flyers to the right people.

Products that are low cost and high turnover will tend to have a broad market. However, you should consider the typical income of residents in the area you're going to target. For example, areas with public housing would be good for a video store to target. The residents in these areas will generally not have a very high disposable income, meaning they are looking for inexpensive home entertainment.

You need to know exactly who you're dealing with, what they're interested in, and what's going to make them buy your product. If you don't know, you're really just taking your chances.

So let's get specific. Who are the people most likely to be interested in your product or service? Here are some guidelines. But remember, you need to be very specific about answering them.

Age: How old are they?

Sex: Are they male or female?

Income: How much do they make?

Where do they live? Are they local, or do they come from miles around to deal with you?

Step 3: Where Do You Want to Drop Your Flyers?

Depending on the product or service, it pays to give a little thought to where you're going to distribute your flyers. In most cases, it's OK to just drop them into the mailboxes of every home or business in your local area. You should give some thought to how far afield you want to drop them.

Be realistic—just because you have one customer who travels 30 miles to deal with you doesn't mean anyone else will be that devoted. Also, think about how far away you're willing to service. This applies especially if you go to your customer, rather than the other way around.

You also have to think about the level of market demand. There may not be enough potential customers in the local area to make the exercise worthwhile. If your product or service has a specific target market, you need to find a way to get to it directly. Just dropping your flyers anywhere is a waste of money. For example, there's no point in randomly putting out 1000 flyers for a retirement village. Most people who read them will have no interest at all. Why not distribute in a suburb where you know many older people live?

The same applies when sending your flyers to businesses. If you're selling large photocopiers, try dropping your flyers to businesses that are larger than average.

This also raises the questions of how to deliver the flyers. You can do it in one of two ways: Directly into mailboxes or in person. The personal approach has the advantage of being different because people will be forced to pay you at least some attention. It can also be twice as annoying. If you're going to do it this way, make sure you try and target your prospects.

Step 4: What Do You Want to Say?

There's often heated debate about which types of flyers work best, but there's never a disagreement about which types don't. I'm sure you can guess which category those with no obvious purpose fall into. For example, if you write a flyer that says, "Hi. My name's Harry. I cut hair. I've been doing it for 12 years," it's unlikely people will call. Your flyer needs to give them a good reason to read, then a great reason to do something about dealing with you.

Your flyer needs to have a clear purpose, and it needs to take people from point A to point B. Point A is your headline, which should identify where they are now. The body of the letter leads them to Point B, which is where you tell them why they should act right now, and how to act.

Most importantly, you need to understand your customers. If you understand their needs, wants, and positions, you can sell almost anything to them. If you nail the appeal and the message, you'll win.

Your flyer must do one of two things: It must provide a solution to a problem they are having right now, or it must introduce them to something new that appeals. If it doesn't do one of these two things, and do it in a very specific and direct way, you need to ask yourself what the flyer is designed to do.

You must decide on whom you want to target, what you want to say to them, and what you want them to do as a result. For instance, if you want 40-year-old mothers to call and order a pizza within the next three days, think about what you need to say to encourage them to do that. What about, "Tired of cooking? Here's how to feed the family for $14.90 tonight." This headline identifies the situation and offers the deal up-front. It takes the prospect from Point A (*Sick of cooking? Here's an alternative*) to Point B (*The alternative is affordable and limited*).

It pays to remember that simply asking people to act now (or for that matter, telling them to act now) is rarely enough. You need to give them a good reason why *now* is the time to do something.

You see, most purchases can be delayed forever. It's one thing to create desire, but it's another to actually get people to part with their cash. Every month, customers have to decide what to spend their money on. It could very realistically be a decision between buying that new washing machine, or putting up with the old one for a little longer and paying the school fees.

Every buyer has priorities. Of course, there are ways to rearrange them. If you offer a special deal on the washing machine, the customer may think, "Well, perhaps I could replace the old washing machine while the offer is on and speak to the school about paying a little late."

The question is, how do you offer a great deal without slicing your profit margin drastically? There's a couple of ways. First, make sure you are selling products or services with a high margin. Often, that's not possible—you simply can't get a high margin on some items. If you have the option of gearing your business towards higher-margin items, do so, as then it's much easier to come up with great deals. If you can't, you need to find items or services that are highly valued by the customer, yet have a low cost. Extra service is an old standby and information booklets are another. Even better are services you can get for free from other businesses. You'll find more details and examples below.

The other thing to bear in mind when writing flyers is the amount of information you should include. If you have to explain too much, perhaps you should look at another method. Of course, this largely depends on the quality of your information and offer. If your headline is, "I have videotapes of what you did behind your husband's back" and your offer is "call me within the next three days and you can have them back," you could fill a whole page front and back—the prospect would read every word.

Generally, though, it's best to keep it short and punchy. The general format is, "Hey you, here's a great deal. Here's why you should take it up, and here's how to do it." If you have to say too much more than that, you should give some thought to whether flyers are the right way to go.

Step 5: How to Write Your Flyer

Now that we've covered the basics, it's time to look at how to create your flyer.

Headline

You need to take some time writing an effective headline. Your headline must instantly identify who you're after, and what it is you're offering. As your flyer may be competing for the attention of your prospect with many others, the key to its success is in the headline. If you want potential clients to read your flyer, you must gain their interest quickly with a great headline and a strong offer.

You will find out more about writing headlines in Part 6. One of the things you need to keep in mind is that the headline needs to take up at least 25 percent of your flyer.

Typefaces

The typeface or font you use in your flyer can make a big difference in the results you achieve. I've discussed this before; the basic principles are the same for flyers, brochures, and newsletters. Remember the two basic types of font? Sans serif fonts don't have the little "feet" at the bottom of each letter.

The most common type of serif font is Times New Roman. While you may like to use different fonts for your headline and body copy, you must be careful not to overdo it. As a general rule you shouldn't use more than two different typefaces on the one flyer.

Point Size

As a general rule 10 or 9 points are ideal.

Body Copy

You only get one chance with potential customers, so you must arouse their curiosity immediately. That means with the very first paragraph. If they're not excited after the first 50 words, they won't read the rest of your flyer.

Use the bare minimum of copy to get your message across. For goodness sake, don't ramble on. But make sure you include enough information to get your readers interested enough to call you, or bring the flyer in. By holding back some information, you make it necessary for them to call you to find out more.

If your copy looks too long, try putting the key ideas from one paragraph into bullet points. Your body copy should tell a story and be easy to read. When you've finished writing it, get someone to look over it and critique it for you. Only make one offer on your flyer, but make it exciting.

Highlighting Text

Use bold type to highlight key points in your body copy, headlines, and subheadlines.

Italics can also be used to highlight key areas of your copy, although it can be hard to read and should be used only sparingly. Never use all capitals. The only time you can is in a short headline, or for extra emphasis.

To make your copy easier to read, break it up into paragraphs. By indenting your paragraphs rather than leaving a line between them, you can cut down on wasted space.

Also consider using a drop cap first letter, as this is a great way to attract the eye of your reader. Try putting your text in columns rather than having it stretched across the page. This breaks your copy down into bite-sized chunks, and makes it easier for the eye to follow.

Subheadlines

Subheadlines have three major benefits:

- They break up large blocks of text, making them easier to read. If your copy looks like one big "chunk" of text, it can put people off. By using subheadlines you can break your copy up and give it some "space."

- They allow readers skimming over your flyer to read only the points that interest them.

- They spark the readers' interest. If your headline doesn't get them in completely, you get a second chance with your subheadlines.

It is important that your subheadlines tell a story. They need to be able to convey your message to those who are just browsing.

Coupons

Coupons are a great way to measure the success of your campaign. If you're not getting coupons back, your flyers are not working. Because many people will only briefly look over your flyer, you need to repeat your offer in the coupon.

People will normally read the headline first, the subheadlines next, and then finally the coupon. You can often get people to go back and read the copy by making a strong, clear offer in your coupon.

Pictures

People will find your flyer far more interesting if you include a few photographs. But just throwing in a few pictures won't work. You need to put some thought into the type of pictures and their positions.

Don't use line drawings or clip art if you can help it. Photographs get a much higher response than illustrations. The only time you may consider using line art is in the form of technical diagrams, or a map to indicate your location.

So what types of photographs are suitable? Photographs of your premises or your product are suitable for use on flyers. The pictures need to back up your story. For example, photographs of people using your product or service. These can be used to educate people on what it is you do, and it can also be a great way to teach people how easy it is to use your product.

Consider putting a photograph of yourself on your flyer. Remember, people buy from people, not companies, so let them see the person behind the company name. Place your photograph so it looks straight out off the page or towards your body copy. If your picture is looking into an ad, your potential customers will also be drawn into it.

Always put a caption under your photograph. Everybody reads the captions, so make sure you take advantage of this opportunity to get them into your ad.

Color

Printing your flyers in color will cost quite a bit more than standard black text on white stock. Bear in mind that the aim of your flyer is to bring customers into your business. The less you spend on attracting them, the better. If your headline promises a benefit, your copy conveys your message, and your offer is worthwhile, it could be argued you have no need for color.

But as we mentioned earlier, your flyer could be competing with many others. You therefore need to ask yourself if your flyer is going to stand out well enough to be read, or will it go straight into the trash can? This is something you should test and measure. Print some in black and white and then see what sort of response they get. If they don't perform well, try the same flyers in color.

If you are going to use any color, you'd be well advised to print in full-process color. Printing on colored paper is an inexpensive way to brighten up your flyer. But be careful which color paper you choose, as it can make your flyer difficult to read. Keep this in mind if you decide to print your text in color. As a general rule you're far better off printing your text in black, as this will increase readability.

Layouts

You'll find a number of effective layouts at the end of this section. Something to keep in mind when you're doing your layout is how easy it is to read and understand. Many people fall into the trap of trying to jazz their flyers up by adding different shapes and elements. My advice is simple: Unless you have a good deal of artistic ability, you're best sticking to a simple layout. Putting your headline at the top, your coupon in the bottom right corner, and your pictures in the middle may not sound exciting, but it will generally bring better results.

Try to do your layout in blocks. By this I mean placing the headline, copy, pictures, and coupon in a blocked, or balanced, layout on the page. Keep your layout tight and don't leave too much empty space on the page. You're paying for these flyers so use every bit of space that you can.

If you want to try something out of the ordinary, you should pay a graphic designer to do it for you. But remember, they can be expensive.

Size

The size of your flyers will depend on how much information you need to include. I would normally recommend you limit yourself to 5.8 × 8.3 inches, or an A5-sized sheet of paper. You probably wouldn't place an ad in the newspaper that was larger than this and so you shouldn't have any problems fitting all you need to say into this space.

- You can fit two flyers on one standard letter size or A4 sheet of paper. This will save you quite a bit in printing costs, as you'll only need half as much paper than you would if you were printing letter on A4.

- You may wish to try odd-sized paper or card. This can certainly make your flyer stand out but again, unless you have great artistic flair, you're best advised to consult a professional designer, printer, or a member of the *Action International* creative team. Having your flyer cut out in unusual shapes can also help attract attention to it.

Stock

As you know, stock is the term used for the type of paper or card that you print your flyers on. There are literally thousands of types for you to choose from, and their prices range accordingly. So before deciding on the type to use for your particular flyer, you need to consider the type of product you're about to promote. You need to understand using a high-quality stock, your prospects will believe that yours is a high-quality product.

Printing

The final consideration in the creation of your flyer is how to have it printed. This will depend largely on your budget, and the type of product you're trying to sell. You basically have three choices:

- Professional printer: This is more expensive but ensures that your flyers will look first-rate. Always have your flyers professionally printed if your budget allows. This is a must for those higher-priced products.

- Personal printer: If you own, or have access to, a good-quality computer printer, you may be able to save on your printing cost. However, you need to keep in mind the quality of the stock you use, and the price of your product. If you're printing a large number of flyers, it would probably work out more cost-effectively in the long run to have them done professionally.

- Photocopies: Only use this option as a last resort. But if you do, make sure the quality of reproduction is high.

One of the ways you may be able to offset the cost of printing is through supplier subsidy. If you're promoting a particular product, you should contact the manufacturers and ask them to assist you with the cost of the promotion. Explain to them what you're trying to achieve, and what it will do for them.

Step 6: When Should You Drop Your Flyers?

If your product is isn't a seasonal one, you don't have to be too concerned about when to drop your flyers. It's more a question of which day, rather than which time of year.

Most businesses drop flyers in the middle of the week, so it may a good idea to avoid those times. Having said that, people are usually less willing to look at advertising material on Fridays, as they just want to clean up and get the weekend under way.

If your business is seasonal, you need to approach flyers differently. For example, a lawn mower shop would find it fruitless dropping a flyer in winter. The business owner would need to adapt the appeal to suit the time of year.

Step 7: What Else Do You Need to Think About?

Use this section as a final checklist. Once you're happy with your flyers, run through and make sure you're ready to get started. Here are a few things you may not have thought of:

Team training: Do your team members fully understand the strategy you've implemented? It's important that they understand the vital role they are to play. If new customers come in and find that things don't quite meet their expectations, your flyer campaign will fail.

Check stock and team levels: It's unlikely your flyer campaign will bring in hundreds of people all at once (very few actually do), but you do need to be prepared, just in case. Imagine losing new customers just because you had no stock or your team was too busy to serve them. Plan for your flyer campaign by making sure you can cater to any increased demand that may arise.

"Charlie, I'm going to leave you with these templates. They'll help you get going when its time to produce your own. Simply choose the design and fill in the words, referring to the notes you made today, of course. It's that simple—and it works. That I personally guarantee."

"Thanks, Brad, I'll certainly be doing my own soon. I think I'll tie them in to an overall promotional strategy that includes a variety of promotional tools. How's that? I'm even beginning to speak like a marketing guru!"

Examples

Here are a few good examples to work through. Have a good look at them and see how the various elements have been handled. It's quite simple once you get the hang of it.

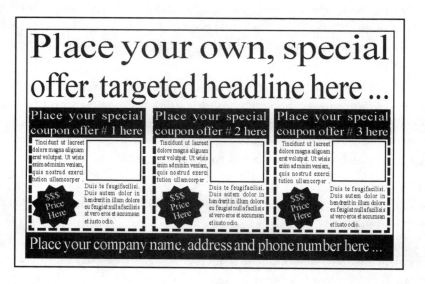

Place your own benefit-filled headline here ...

Place your subheadline here. This should explain any key points that you couldn't fit in your headline.

Hekng edlgndf dflnad hrh gnn gbn adf. Osh fgnu kty dh ryjLorem ipsum dolor sit amet, consectetuer adipiscing elit, sed diem nonummy nibh euismod tincidunt ut lacreet dolore magna aliguam erat volutpat. Ut wisis enim ad minim veniam, quis nostrud exerci tution ullamcorper suscipit lobortis nisl ut aliquip ex ea commodo consequat. Duis te feugifacilisi. Duis autem dolor in hendrerit in vulputate velit esse molestie consequat, vel illum dolore eu feugiat nulla facilisis at vero eros et accumsan et iusto odio.

Place a photograph here.

Place your Company Name Your Company Address and your Company Phone Number here.

Repeat your offer here

Name ....

Address ....

....

Place your company name, address, and phone number here.

Place your own benefit filled headline here ...

Place your sub-headline here. This should explain any key points that you couldn't fit in your headline.

1. Hekng edlgndf dflnad
hrh gnn gbn adf. Osh fgnu kty dh ryjLorem ipsum dolor sit amet, consectetuer adipiscing elit, sed diem nonummy nibh euismodde

2. Hekng edlgndf dflnad
hrh gnn gbn adf. Osh fgnu kty dh ryjLorem ipsum dolor sit amet, consectetuer adipiscing elit, sed diem nonummy nibh euismodde

3. Hekng edlgndf dflnad
hrh gnn gbn adf. Osh fgnu kty dh ryjLorem ipsum dolor sit amet, consectetuer adipiscing elit, sed diem nonummy nibh euismodde

4. Hekng edlgndf dflnad
hrh gnn gbn adf. Osh fgnu kty dh ryjLorem ipsum dolor sit amet, consectetuer adipiscing elit, sed diem nonummy nibh euismodde

Place a "what's on", or special offer headline here

Tincidunt ut lacreet dolore magna aliguam erat volutpat. Ut wisis enim ad minim veniam, quis nostrud exerci tution ullamcorper . Duis te feugifacilisi. Duis autem dolor in hendrerit in illum dolore eu feugiat nulla facilisis at vero eros et accumsan et iusto odio.

Repeat your offer here

Name ....

Address ....

Place your company name, address and phone number here.

Place your own targeted headline here ...

Tincidunt ut lacreet dolore magna aliguam erat volutpat. Ut wisis enim ad minim veniam, quis. Tincidunt ut lacreet dolore veniam, quis nostrud exerci tution ullamcorper . Duis ryjr r ryuy i iopu iote feugifacilisi. Duis autem dolor in hendrerit in illum dolore eu feugiat nulla facilisis at vero eros et accumsan et iusto odio. Tincidunt ut lacreet dolore magna aliguam erat volutpat. Ut wisis enim ad minim veniam, quis nostrud exerci tution ullamcorper . Duis te feugifacilisi. Tincidunt ut lacreet dolore magna aliguam erat volutpat. Ut wisis enim ad minim magna aliguam erat volutpat. Ut wisis enim ad minim veniam, quis nostrud exerci tution ullamcorper . Duis te feugifacilisi.

Company Name
Address
Phone Number

Royal Bank of Company Name Date 00/00/00

Please Pay _____

The amount of _____

This cheque entitles the bearer to (offer).
This cheque is not redeemable in cash.

$ 00.00

Part 5

∎ Business Cards and Letterheads

Consider this section your do-it-yourself guide to creating business cards that bring you more business, and letterheads that actually make you more sales.

Once you've worked your way through this part of the book, you should know exactly how to design business stationery that looks good, but more importantly, that does some good for your bottom line. On top of that, you'll have the drafts of your new business cards and letterheads complete, ready to take to the printers.

But let's return to Charlie's Garage for the time being.

"Charlie, what I'm going to do now is to take you, step-by-step, through the process of designing your new stationery. I'm going to start right at the beginning, from deciding on colors and typefaces, right through to how to get the best deals on printing and duplication."

"No worries, Brad. I guess you've noticed how boring my letterheads are."

"No, I'm not criticizing your business, Charlie. Understand this: Your letterheads and business cards form part of your image and as such, paying close attention to them can affect how your business is perceived by prospects and customers alike. This means that they are another important promotional tool that you can use to your benefit. Does that make sense?"

"Yes, perfectly. Oddly enough, I had been planning to revamp my letterhead. So, I guess there's no better time than now, is there?"

"As the old saying goes, there's no time like the present. So, shall we start?"

"Lead the way, Brad."

"Once you really begin to think about it, you'll be surprised at how much you can do with your business stationery. When you throw off the conventional ideas concerning the "way it should be done," there is a whole world of opportunity that most business owners never capitalize on.

"Remember, it's your business and you can run it the way you want. Just because none of your competitors take a particular approach, there's no reason why you shouldn't be the maverick who does it first. In fact, there's probably every reason why you should."

"Do you mean that, Brad?"

"Absolutely. Why shouldn't you do with your business whatever you feel is right for it? That's the beauty of it—try something new, see how it goes, and then tweak it, change it, or reinforce it. It's rather like fixing a car. What happens when someone brings in a car and says to you it isn't running properly?"

"I'd first run the engine and listen to it myself. Then, depending on what I feel, I'd run a few basic checks to see if I can isolate the problem. I'd start with the carburetor, then if that seems OK, I'd check the ignition system. If that's OK, I'd look at the timing, and so on until I find the problem. When I do, I'll fix it."

"Business is essentially the same, Charlie. We initially decide on a strategy to correct a challenge we are facing. Let's say it's a challenge with promoting the business. If it is, we could decide to design a brochure, for instance. Or we could opt for new stationery. We'd then design something and test and measure the results in a pilot program first before deciding whether it works or not. If it does, we then implement it on a larger, and more expensive, scale. If we find it doesn't work, we'd think about trying a different strategy, like a newsletter or brochure. Get it?"

"You're preaching to the converted, Brad. You're talking my language. And I always thought I was just a mechanic! How wrong I was. I'm actually a businessman!"

"That's absolutely right, Charlie. It's important to approach this subject with an open mind, and be ready to try new things. Forget everything you know and start afresh. Everything I'm going to tell you has already been proven to work with other businesses, and these ideas will work for you too."

Charlie's situation is typical of many I've worked on over the years. It's being able to recognize where you're at, businesswise, having the courage to make the decision to do something about it, and then having the will to take *Action*. And remember, there's never been a better time than now to start.

So, this is the next step in your marketing success story. From this point on, you'll have the skills to create business stationery that makes a big difference to your business.

You'll be pleased to know that you don't have to be a great writer, or a graphic designer—it's all laid out in an easy-to-read format, and with lots of simple examples to bring you up to speed.

Best of all, you'll find templates of business cards and letterheads at the end of this section. These are "fill-in-the-blanks" examples of how to design your new business stationery. These examples have already worked for plenty of businesses, and they'll certainly work for you. All you need to do is insert the relevant information (your business name, contact number, e-mail address, etc.), and you'll have *instant* business cards and letterheads.

This is truly the best part. Even if the main content leaves you confused, you'll still be able to use the templates. These are designed for people who want someone else to do all the thinking!

Of course, it's in your best interests to do a little of your own thinking too. Remember, the more thought you give it, the more sales you'll see at the end of the day. And ultimately, that's the great thing about being in business for yourself—if you work smarter, you see more money! When you're in a job, working smarter often isn't even noticed.

Although it may be tempting to just flick over to the templates, fill in the blanks and carry on with life, it's highly recommended that you take the time and read the text word for word. Not only will you find important information on creating your new stationery, but also you'll be quite surprised by how much you learn about your business.

OK, let's get started. Open your mind, and get ready to work.

Testing and Measuring

Testing and measuring are the most important aspects of any marketing activity that you do for your business. It's important that you track how much you're spending and how much you're seeing back.

Remember, it's always better to hand out 20 business cards that don't work, than 20,000. Even if you love your new stationery, and everyone who sees it goes crazy, it's important to keep your head, and avoid going too far too soon.

Take it slow at first, check the response, then gradually increase the numbers. You have the option of creating a number of versions of your business cards and letterheads, and trying each version at the same time. Ask people where they heard about you, and which business card they have. Over time, you may notice that one version seems to do much better than the others. This is the one that you keep.

The problem is, creating business cards and letterheads can be expensive—there are the setup costs, then the printing costs. If you were to create multiple versions of both, you'd end up spending quite a deal more than if you just decided on one and stuck to it.

Ultimately, it depends on how important business cards and letterheads are to your business. If they represent one of your most crucial sources of new business and repeat sales, then it may be in your best long-term interests to pay for two different sets of stationery.

When doing this, it's best to keep some continuity between the two versions. Obviously, retain the same basic look (logo and in general, the colors too). There's no real benefit in completely confusing people with two entirely different visual images.

The other option is to create a small number (about 20) of each version you're thinking about using. Show these to as many people as you can—customers, friends, family. When they give you feedback, *listen* to what they have to say. Don't block out their criticism of your favorite design, or minimize their praise of the one you didn't like.

It pays to not be precious about it—this isn't fine art we're talking about. Your stationery is a business tool that is designed to make you money. Take note of what people say, and act accordingly.

What Is Success?

This isn't a section that will answer any great philosophical questions. It's all about knowing when you have designed business stationery that really works, and when you haven't.

If you aren't sure what you're aiming for, it's difficult to achieve it. Before you even getting started, it's a good idea to consider what's possible, and have an understanding of what isn't.

Once you do, you then have a framework to work with. "OK, we'd like 1 in every 10 people we give business cards to, to become regular customers."

Let's deal with the two elements of your new business stationery separately.

Business Cards

How many business cards have you accumulated in your life? 20? 100? 300?

For most people (especially business owners), the answer would range well into the hundreds. The tendency for salespeople to give out business cards to basically anyone is rife. In fact, just as with a brochure, handing out a business card is often a substitute for making a sale. They think, "I couldn't be bothered closing this sale, so I'll just hand out a business card and wait for them to call me—at least that way I've done something."

This kind of thinking is precisely the same as letting customers walk out when they say, "I want to think about it—I'll be back."

Come on! How many of these customers ever come back? I'd be amazed if the ratio was any higher than 1 in 20.

Most business owners and their staff abuse business cards. They're treated as a kind of "good-bye" device, and they rarely achieve anything.

By the same token, they're also very valuable tools. A business card is, theoretically, a mobile advertisement for your business that works continuously.

Every time the customers open their wallets, you're right there, offering a reminder that you exist.

There are two important things to consider:

- Is there anything about your business card that gives customers a reason to hang onto it? Is it anything more than just a statement of your business name and contact details? If customers want to contact you again, they'll hang onto it. If they're not sure, they'll probably throw it away.

- Does it encourage the customer to call you? Does it actually *sell* for you? Perhaps you're thinking that a business card can't sell. Wrong! A business card can sell like nothing else.

The important thing to remember is that a business card is nothing more than a miniflyer, a little advertisement that can fit in someone's wallet or purse. It's like giving someone one of your flyers and saying, "Here, hang onto this."

So, how do you know when your business card is working?

You have to ask people where they heard about you. If you keep hearing, "I have one of your business cards," you're getting a fair indication that your cards are being retained and used.

The other way to know is this by putting a special offer on your business card that you don't advertise anywhere else. For example, you could have a line on your card that says, "The first time you visit, present this card for a 25 percent discount."

If you use the offer approach, make an offer that people will want to come in for. Just saying "5 percent discount" or something similarly minuscule is usually not enough to get people excited (unless you sell a really big-ticket item, like new homes).

The main aim is to have people keep your business card and refer back to it the next time that they need whatever it is you sell.

A brilliant way to improve your chances of this is by putting a table of important information on the back of the card. For example, if you sell houses, why not include a "mortgage rate calculator" on the back. There are plenty of other options you could use along the same lines.

If people are just taking your card, then filing it away in a huge business card folder, you're probably not seeing much return. The card should be *used*.

Shortly you'll discover how to make your card appealing enough to be held onto, and how to make sure it gets used every time that the customer needs to buy what you sell.

On a purely financial level, it's worth considering how much you're spending on your cards, and how much you expect to see back in actual sales. Business cards are no different than any other marketing device. You have only so much to spend on marketing and you have to decide where to spend it—if business cards are less cost-effective than newspaper advertising, you may be smarter diverting the funds to the newspaper, rather than the printer.

It pays to remember the idea of lifetime value when considering the cost-effectiveness of your business cards.

Lifetime value is the amount customers are worth to you over the course of their lifetimes. If they come back and visit four times a year, and spend $300 each time, their lifetime value will be $1200 multiplied by how many years they keep coming back.

If you have to hand out $1200 worth of business cards to attract this one customer, then it will take you a year before you see a positive return on investment (assuming very high profit margins).

If the customer turns out to be a very loyal one who returns year after year, and refers lots of friends, it's probably been a good business decision to hand out those 10,000 business cards. Of course, if your business cards only attract one customer for every 10,000 cards you hand out, you'd probably want to seriously consider redesigning them.

Letterheads

Most business owners never even consider using their letterheads as selling tools. They think that their letterheads should be nothing more than statements of their business names and contact details.

As with business cards, the opposite is true—your letterhead should tell people why they should buy from you. You have their attention, so why not take the opportunity and hit them with your four best-selling points (for example) then and there?

It's important to remember that you are not obligated to do things a certain way—you are making the rules, so you decide how it will be. If you want to put pictures of 20 staff members on your letterhead, then you are welcome to.

You need to think about what you want your letterhead to achieve. It pays to keep in mind that customers have no expectations of your letterhead. They don't have any predetermined notion of what they expect to see there.

So how do you know when you're making the very best use of your letterhead?

Unlike business cards, it's trickier to measure the success of a letterhead design. In general, it won't offer you any direct results to test and measure. You have to be a little shrewder in determining its effectiveness. By that, I mean you have to be more sensitive to the reactions of your customers and potential new clients.

One option is to use your letterhead as an opportunity to list all your services. You might even go as far as listing prices. If customers start calling up for other services in addition to those they normally get, you could probably draw the conclusion that your letterhead is having an effect.

The same could be said if you change your letterhead and start seeing a dramatic improvement in the response to your direct mail letters. Let's say you're getting a 3 percent response to a particular letter. If you change your letterhead, yet keep the letter exactly the same, and then start getting a 5 percent response, you could reasonably conclude that the letterhead is having an impact.

See, the letterhead can be used to add credibility to your main selling message. For example, if you're send out lots of quotes, it can be a great idea to list the four reasons to buy from you on your letterhead (for this approach, you'd probably put the letterhead down the right hand side of the page). This way, people get the price information, plus a strong selling message. The best part about this approach is that every time you write to them, you'll be hammering home your strongest selling points. If you write to customers four times in a year, they'll ultimately be very familiar with the reasons that they should deal with you.

The Four Steps to Creating Your New Business Cards and Letterheads

Step 1: What Do You Want To Say?

The first thing to work out is the text that will appear on your business cards and letterheads. But before you do, you need to decide on the most important aspects of your business—the key benefits and selling points that people will be interested in.

There are really three ways to go:

1. **Five Reasons:** This is where you print the five reasons to deal with you on the back of your business card and down the side of your letterhead. You include a headline ("five reasons you should deal with us every time you need x") and then simply list the main benefits of dealing with your business. For example, number 1 might be "Lowest prices guaranteed—if you can find an item cheaper anywhere else in Sydney, we'll knock a further 10 percent off that price." Number 2 could be "The best service anywhere—we don't employ anyone unless they've worked in the industry for at least six years. That means every staff member knows a *lot,* and can answer any question you have. We don't have special experts—we're all experts." This approach works particularly well because it's easy to write and very easy to read. It's not difficult to come up with the five things that set you apart.

2. **USP:** This stands for Unique Selling Proposition. Your USP is the one thing that is truly different about you, or at least the one thing that you can promote as being different. Remember, a successful USP should be:

   - Truly unique

   - Exciting to your target market

   - Something that will get people talking

   - Something that can't be easily copied, or if it can, it will be an obvious rip-off on the part of the offending business

   To really get to grips with discovering your competitive advantage and uniqueness, read my book *Instant Leads.*

What about your business? When you started, did you begin with a uniqueness, a real point of difference, or did you just start as a "me-too" competitor? Understand this: To survive in business today, you must *stand out*. If you have no uniqueness, you have no reason for existence. Remember that, as new competitors come into the market, you'll continue to sink. If there's no reason to continue coming to you, and not them, you'll keep losing customers. It's a gloomy forecast, but a realistic one. So list down everything you do that could be considered even a little bit unique. These points don't have to be earth shattering—just different enough to matter.

Basically, your uniqueness comes from one of seven areas: quality, price, service, delivery, speed, convenience, and experience. In case you're wondering, "experience" means the actual experience of buying from you. Imagine a video store that has four 11-foot screens that constantly play the latest releases, and has live entertainment all day and night. That would be a real experience, wouldn't it?

Once you've decided on your uniqueness, it's time to write it down. This is important because your USP will soon be communicated to your team and your customers. It needs to be summed up by a one- or two-line statement. Think "Always Coca Cola" or "Toyota: Oh, What a feeling." There's nothing wrong with this USP: "Jim's Video—the only video store in Wollongong with four 11-foot screens playing the latest releases and all-day live entertainment."

Just state your uniqueness plainly and simply. It's great to be specific. If you can put a number in your USP, that's ideal. Think about the "11 herbs and spices," or the "32 flavors." These are USPs that stick in your mind. A beautician could say "Beauty Shoppe: 4 qualified and friendly beauticians with more than 23 years of experience each."

It may be an idea to write your USP in a long form first, then pick out the best points and turn it into one short and punchy sentence.

Now, it's time to write yours. Don't worry too much about the wording, just get the point across. If you show it to people and they don't seem to understand, you may want to rethink it. If they seem to get the idea immediately, you're on the right track.

Once you've determined your USP, the next step is easy. You print it on everything, especially your business cards and letterheads.

The back of your business card might simply be a statement of your USP and a small explanation. For example, "Harry's Hardware—where every member of our staff used to be a tradesman. Our team of hardware experts knows hardware inside and out. That's because they've used it every day of their working lives. Whether you're a carpenter, plumber, electrician, builder, or a home handyman, you'll find someone to relate to at Harry's Hardware."

Actually, there's nothing wrong with printing the very same thing on your letterheads, word for word. Remember, people don't care what you put there—they'll accept anything as normal.

You have the choice of whether to leave the space blank, or whether to include a message that will increase the chances of people's buying from you. If you are going to take the USP approach, it needs to be strong. You can't just say, "Harry's Hardware—where the service is good." People won't have any reaction to that, and anyone can claim it. But not everyone can claim that their entire team of employees used to be tradespeople. The important thing is, customers of a hardware store would probably care about this type of thing, and the USP would give them a reason to shop at Harry's and *not* somewhere else.

Remember, if you own a hardware store offering "good service" as your USP, and there is another hardware store offering "good service" as theirs, customers have no reason to shop at either place in preference to the other. Make your USP something worth reading, and then print it boldly on your business cards and letterheads.

3. **Guarantee and Photo:** The third approach you can take with your business card and letterhead text is the guarantee and photo idea. Basically, you simply put a photo of yourself and your name (assuming you are the business owner/managing director) and then print a caption that says, "I personally guarantee . . ."

A successful and powerful guarantee should be:

- Specific
- Something that addresses the main frustrations and fears of customers when dealing with your industry
- Complete—it should say either this happens or we'll do that
- Impressive

People have been burned before—they've used products they were told were fantastic, only to be bitterly disappointed. You must take that risk away for them. To delve deeper into this subject, read my book *Instant Leads*.

If you guarantee to give people the benefit that they are after in the first place, there is a good chance they'll want to deal with you. Imagine a hotel resort that had a special guarantee on one of their holidays that read like this: "If you don't feel 100% relaxed after our five-day tropical retreat holiday, we'll offer you one night's accommodation free!"

Remember, people aren't just buying a place to sleep; they are buying a retreat from their day-to-day life. It's all about understanding what makes the customers tick, then absolutely guaranteeing to give them that. If they don't feel that they have received what you promised, they get compensation. When people feed they have nothing to lose, they are more likely to buy and take action. Most action is delayed forever, simply because people are afraid of what will happen if they make a mistake.

A guarantee can short-circuit the sale process too. If people already feel certain that they will get what they set out to get, they will be less worried about spending time procrastinating over every detail. If there's ever a problem, they know that they can come back and see you and get their money back. Of course, you need to make sure that the product you are recommending is the right one for their needs. And naturally, if your product or service isn't up to snuff, a guarantee may kill your business. However, if 98 percent of your customers are happy, and you are satisfied with your product or service, then guarantee away. If people always seem to be happy, why not guarantee that they will be?

So what should you guarantee, and how should you write it?

The best way is to completely forget about what you can do—let's think about what your customers want. Once you know what they want, let's work out how you can promise to give it to them.

OK, to begin with, let's work out the biggest frustration customers have when dealing with you. Think about it: What really bugs your customers? Now, how can you guarantee to overcome that for them? Of course, that one thing may not be achievable—you have to ask yourself whether it's economically viable. OK, if you can't do the first one, let's move on to the next biggest frustration. Think about it: What else bugs your customers?

Now let's develop a guarantee based on that. Can't be done? Move onto the next one, but make sure you're giving each one a fair chance of success. Once you know what you want to guarantee, it's time to write it down. This will be promoted on all of your business cards and your letterhead, so it pays to take the time with it.

The basic format for a powerful guarantee is simple: "If this doesn't happen, then we'll do that." For example: a no-win, no-fee policy from a personal injury lawyer. "If you don't win, we don't get paid." How much business is that guarantee going to get that lawyer?

Now it's time to write yours. First, write the first part of your guarantee—this is where you promise that something will happen. Make the actual promise as specific as you can. Put a time frame on it and make it really stand out. Explain what will happen—the real benefit of buying the product or service. Second, write the "this-will-happen" bit—don't be afraid of the money back, or a "we'll keep working with you until you get the results" guarantee.

Another option is, "we'll pay for you to see our most hated competitor," or "we'll write you a check for the amount you invested plus $1000 to go to your favorite charity." Now that's powerful! Of course, it depends on the industry.

Under your photo and name, you write, "I personally guarantee you will [promise]. If not, we will [what will happen]."

The beauty of the photo is that it makes you seem a lot more credible. People subconsciously think, "Well, if he's willing to put his photo and name to it, it must be the real deal."

The photo should be a head and shoulders shot of yourself smiling, and dressed the way you'd normally be dressed if you were at work. Look straight ahead and smile.

Once you've decided on your approach, the rest is very simple. Most important is understanding your customers. If you understand their needs, wants, and position, it's very easy to write text that will appeal to them. If you nail the "appeal" and the message, you'll win.

The other thing to bear in mind when writing the text for your business card and letterhead is the amount of information you should include. If you feel you need an letter-sized business card just to get the message across, perhaps you should look at another approach. Usually, you only have the back of the business card to make your point, although you might consider doing a "double-folded" business card, giving you three full panels to work with (one for the logo and business details, the rest for selling).

It's never a good idea to squash hundreds of words in a small font size on the back of your cards. They won't get read. You're better off using a bigger font size and saying a lot less.

The same goes for letterheads. Whether you decide to put your letterhead at the top, the bottom, or down the side of the page, it's important that there's plenty of white space. The letterhead needs to be distinct from the rest of the information on the page, and white space is the best way to achieve this.

Remember, your business cards and letterheads should just give the main reasons to deal with you. It may be one very good reason (a USP or guarantee) or a list of things that will appeal (the five-reasons approach).

Because you have only a limited number of words to play with, you need to make the most of every one. That doesn't mean you need to be a great writer who knows how to craft every sentence to perfection. It just means you should say things in the shortest way possible.

Once you've written your text, go back through it and knock out any words that don't need to be there. If you're not certain whether a sentence is necessary, take it out altogether, then see if everything still makes sense.

Your customers aren't that interested in reading a novel down the side of your letterhead, or turning over your business card to read beautifully constructed prose that could be published as poetry. They just want the facts—the key reasons why they should call you.

It's a good idea to keep in mind that people don't really care about you or your business. That might sound harsh, but it's true. People care about themselves, their friends, and their happiness. Where they get their hair cut or which video store they choose doesn't really make that much difference to them.

Your business cards and letterheads just need to get the point across quickly and succinctly so the customer thinks, "Okay, these guys seem all right."

It's really as simple as that.

Step 2: How Do You Want Your Stationery to Look?

There are people out there who get paid hundreds of thousands of dollars every year to design "visual images" for companies and businesses. These are people who talk about logos and corporate colors as if it's some kind of art form, and that their designs express something really profound and deep.

The truth is, if the logos of the big corporations are really saying something important about the "heart and soul" of the company, it goes right over the head of 99.9999 percent of the population. People just don't care about things like that, and why should they?

When it comes to designing your stationery, forget about art and all this abstract nonsense. Just put it right out of your mind, because it will only lead you down the garden path.

Again, I once dealt with a client who decided to make a horse the focus of her logo and business cards. Her business was corporate sales training. When I asked her why she chose a horse as her image, she said, "Horses have always been a big part of my life, and I wanted a logo that got that across."

I found it hard to keep a straight face.

Obviously, she is the only person who cares about her interest in horses. The corporations considering contracting for sales training don't give a damn. The cutesy horse logo was more confusing than anything else, and did nothing to add to the appeal of her business.

She had plenty of justification for the logo—she believed that horses were swift and noble, exactly the qualities she could teach salespeople. It all sounded like rubbish to me, and just a convenient justification for including a horse on her business cards. If she'd just said, "I like horses," and left it at that, I'd probably have had more respect for the idea. It's her business, after all.

Having said that, it's important to note that different colors, images, and fonts give people different impressions. Subconsciously, we associate different looks with different ideas. For example, if you used an old Gothic typeface, people would think of you as classic, steeped in tradition, and maybe of British heritage. If you used a computer-style typeface, people might see you as modern and up-to-date.

The thing is, you don't need any special education to work this stuff out—you already know it. If an image suggests something to you, it's very likely it will suggest the same thing to most people too.

For example, think about lions. If you had a stylized logo on your business cards and letterhead, it would portray a sense of the established. Perhaps even something regal. If you used a dolphin, it would suggest intelligence; it may even have a New Age connotation.

Of course, you're not limited just to animals. Perhaps you could use a musical note, a big tree, or a lightning bolt. All of these things, when tied in with the right word, give a very definite feeling.

For most businesses though, there's no real need to include anything aside from a basic logo. Unless there is an extra visual image that you feel really represents you, and will very positively add to the impression customers get, it's best to leave the idea alone.

Think about the classic logos: McDonald's, Coca-Cola, Levis, Ford, or Shell.

In most cases, these logos mean nothing in particular. The way they're written, the colors, the typeface—it's all subjective.

Of course, there are some people who'd tell you that the Coke logo suggests fun, yet retains a sense of being classic. I'm not really sure, and I'd leave that kind of interpretation up to those more artistically inclined. From a businessperson's point of view, one thing is clear: These logos have succeeded because they have been consistent. They have kept the same basic look since the start, with very slight changes being made very gradually.

Think about McDonald's. They have claimed a very particular red and yellow combination as their own. I remember a billboard campaign they ran some years ago. The billboards were painted red and yellow, and just said "400 yards ahead." As I recall, the ads didn't even contain the distinctive "M" logo. It didn't matter a bit—everyone knew what the ads were for.

When it comes to your logo and look, it's a good idea to stay down-to-earth. Don't get carried away with image and art. Just create a logo and look that represent you accurately.

For example, a business that specialises in handcrafting exquisite wrought iron fencing would use an old-style font and very tasteful colors, probably black and red. If the business broke the mold and used a really modern typeface, a picture of skyscraper, and used bright yellow and green as its main colors, people would get a completely different impression of the business.

Let's deal with each aspect, one at a time.

Typefaces

The two basic types are sans serif and serif fonts. Sans serif fonts don't have the little "feet" at the bottom of each letter. Studies have shown that people find these fonts more difficult to read than serif fonts. This is not really a concern when crafting a logo; it has more impact when writing a long block of text.

When selecting a font, I'd suggest you get on a computer, type your business name, and then experiment with different fonts. Once you've been through 20 or so, pick the three you like best and show it around to different people for their opinions.

Pictures and Drawings

As mentioned before, it's best to avoid drawing and pictures if you're not entirely sure what impact the visual will have on your image. In general, a drawing works better than a picture. A picture just seems too real, or not artistic enough. Unless you're a great artist, it's best to get a professional to draw it for you.

Color

Printing your material in color will cost quite a bit more than standard black text on white paper. More often than not though, it will be worth the money as color definitely adds professionalism. Printing your letterhead on colored paper is an inexpensive way to brighten it up. But be careful which color you choose, as it can make the information you print on it difficult to read.

Layout

You'll find a number of effective layouts at the end of this section. Many people fall into the trap of trying to jazz up their stationery by throwing in lots of different shapes and elements. Unless you have a good deal of artistic ability, you're best sticking with a simpler layout. If you want to try something out of the ordinary, you should ask a graphic designer to design it for you.

When it comes to business cards, it's generally a good idea to put your details (and a photo of the person named on the card) on the front, and your selling message on the back. The photo is often a good idea, as it personalizes the card and makes it stand out.

With letterheads, I'd recommend running the information down the side. This allows you to include more information while keeping the letterhead clearly separated from the rest of the text.

Size

Importantly for business cards (letterheads are always standard sized and don't need to be discussed), your card must fit neatly into a wallet or business card folder. I've discarded plenty of business cards because they were too big for my wallet. I couldn't store them with ease, so I threw them away. Regardless of how well they were printed, there was no way I could hang onto them.

When creating your cards, make sure you ask the printer for a sample, and then test it. If it's too big, don't even consider going ahead until you've adjusted the size. I can't stress this strongly enough.

You may want to consider a double business card that folds over. These can work exceptionally well, especially when the second part of the card contains a tear-off offer. For example, the second part could be presented for a 20 percent discount, or something for free.

Stock

Stock is the term used for the type of paper or card that you print on. Before deciding on the type to use for your stationery, you need to consider the type of product you're about to promote.

If you're selling expensive, good-quality products, it's better to use good-quality stock. For a cheap, consumable product or service, cheaper stock is fine. People generally aren't that concerned, but they may find it strange if your high-quality business promotes itself using the cheapest and thinnest card available.

Step 3: Where Should You Get Them Printed?

Once you've designed your stationery and decided on the stock to use, you then have to decide where and how to get it printed. This will depend largely on your budget. You basically have three choices:

Professional printer: This is more expensive but ensures that your stationery will look first-rate. Always have your stationery professionally printed if your budget allows. Also, you should shop around for a printer who offers a very cheap letterhead and business card package. Most printers are willing to take a loss the first time, because they know that you'll come back for reprints.

Personal printer: If you own, or have access to, a good-quality computer printer, you may be able to save on your printing cost. However you need to keep in mind the quality of the stock you use and the price of your product. If you were printing a large number of letterheads, it would probably be more cost-effective in the long run to have them printed professionally.

Photocopies: This is the bargain basement of printing. If you decide to go with this option, make sure that the quality of reproduction is high. Having black lines all over your stationery will make you, and your product, look cheap and nasty. Only use this option as a last resort, and only for black and white. Color photocopying will always work out to be very expensive.

Step 4: How Should You Use Them?

Once you've produced your stationery, it's time to get it to work for you. Aside from all the usual methods of using business cards (giving them out to customers, friends, and family, and attaching them to your mailouts), you might also like to consider networking. This is especially relevant if most of your customers are other businesses.

The idea of networking strikes fear into the hearts of most businesspeople. Regardless of how old you are, or how good you are at your job, there's a natural tendency to feel a little shy.

Networking has negative connotations—it implies pretending to be something you're not. Nothing could be further from the truth. Networking is purely about introducing yourself to other business owners in a relaxed social setting. It should be (gasp) fun!

I once worked with a financial planner who based his whole business on networking. Every two weeks, he'd invite two clients to dinner, and asked that they invite three business friends each. Now, believe me, this financial planner was no "life of the party." In fact, I'd have to be honest and say he was a little boring and eccentric—completely off in his own world of investments and insurance.

Anyway, the nights went especially well—the financial planner paid for the whole night. It worked out to about $300 per dinner, around the cost of the ads he used to run.

The structure of the night was always the same. Introductions and name badges, a brief talk by all of the guests (what they did, who they were, etc), a light entree, a 30-minute presentation by the financial planner on a topic, then dinner and conversation. He gave everyone business cards, and got business cards in return.

The next day he would follow each person up on the phone. He didn't lie and pretend that he now wanted to become best friends (that would have turned people off right away). He'd simply say, "Would you like to meet and work out how we can set something up for you?"

Essentially, this became the only marketing or promotion he did. It cost him $300 every two weeks, but he made two new clients from each dinner party almost every time. Over the lifetime of the client, he saw the acquisition cost ($150) back many, many times over.

His business cards were better than the average too. They listed "5 reasons why I'm the best financial planner you'll ever meet." People thought that was a little cocky, but he had the experience to back up his claims.

Between the dinner and the time he called, they'd had time to look at his business card, and read through the information it contained. It was like a miniflyer. And he made lots of new friends to boot. Even some of the people who didn't come on board started inviting him out to their parties and networking nights. He was introduced to lots of new people, and thus made even more contacts that turned into sales.

Of course, he didn't need to pay for the dinner. He could have invited people along and ask them to pay $20 for four drinks and a meal. He could have even struck up a great deal with the restaurant, and gotten commission for introducing these eight people as new customers. If he went to the same restaurant every time, he'd eventually be able to get an amazing deal, and maybe even make a profit out of the dinner alone. It's amazing what can happen when you start thinking this way.

Now I want you to keep in mind, this guy was certainly not Mr. Personality, and if the truth be known, he was often very nervous before the dinners. He worked around that by shifting the focus to his guests, letting everyone have a few drinks, talking about something he really knew about, and saving the main conversation until everyone had eaten and loosened up a little. The pressure was never really on.

Dinner with clients and their friends is one way to network. Let's look at a few others:

The Sports Club

This is by far my favorite. When you get involved with a golf club, you'll almost always find that you run into plenty of people who own their own businesses. You don't have to go into it with the express purpose of making contacts. Just aim to have a good time, improve your swing, and meet some people. Whenever you have a beer with people at the clubhouse, or play a round with business owners, slip them a card. Even if they thought you were quirky, they'll still trust you beyond any other supplier of your type. Personal contact means everything. If they've shared one beer and had a laugh with you, they'll prefer you to almost anyone. It's easy, fun, and it really does work.

Business after Hours

If you go scouting around, you'll find that someone in your area organizes regular networking nights. It's like a whole other world, but not hard to break into at all. People go there to meet other people (like a singles' bar). They expect to talk to you, and to find out what you do. Obviously, they are there to make contacts themselves, but they'll happily listen to you talk about why you're so different and so good. If they believe you, they may even become a client. Watch out though. You may see a few of your colleagues there doing the same thing. These Business after Hours nights are prime hunting grounds for business owners who deal with other businesses.

One other thing that's most important: You should use your letterhead at every opportunity. Even if you're just mailing out an invoice, why not print it on your letterhead? The more consistently that you use it, the more familiar people will become with your key benefits. Every time they get something from you, they will be subconsciously absorbing your selling message.

"We've covered a lot today, Charlie. I'm going to leave it there for today. But what I'd like you to do is come up with a concept for your own letterhead and business card. Do you think you can do that?"

"For sure, Brad. I have some ideas already that I'm dying to try. Mind if I shoot them over to your office tomorrow once I've had a play around on the computer?"

"No worries. Look forward to seeing them."

We shook hands, set a date for our next meeting, and walked out to where my car was parked. The session had been extremely fruitful, and Charlie was more motivated than ever.

I knew he'd begin experiencing results very shortly.

Examples

True to his word, Charlie delivered his drafts to my office the next day. This is what he produced:

Part 6

▌Writing "Killer" Headlines

Writing a headline for a promotional tool is very similar to writing one for an advertisement. Both headlines need to sell. Sometimes they sell a product or service; other times they sell ideas. So let's look at a few basic considerations:

Press Releases

The headline for your press release must "sell" journalists or editors on the idea that what you've sent them is a worthwhile story. Just as an advertisement's headline needs to grab the readers attention, so too does the headline for your press release. The newsroom of any media outlet is a hectic place. There are many story ideas to be covered on any one day, and only the best will make it to print or air.

As I've mentioned before, one of the easiest ways for you to get a feel for writing effective headlines is to buy a number of newspapers or magazines and copy their style. Alternatively, if you're writing for radio or television, listen to the types of opening lines they use at the start of their news stories, and try to write in a similar way.

Remember, the headline you write will probably not be the one they'll use. Editors and production managers will normally change your headline to one that reflects the direction they want the story to take. Of course, this doesn't always have to be the case. If the headline you write is good enough for the job, they will more than likely run with it. This, of course, has the advantage of making their life easier, and increasing the chances of your story being accepted.

Writing headlines for different types of stories and businesses requires slightly different styles. If you're writing for a retail store, your headline will be different than that if you were writing for a manufacturing firm. You also need to keep in mind where your story is to run, and whether or not you want it to be factual or antagonistic.

Think you can do it? Let's give it a try, then. Shortly you'll practice writing "killer" headlines in 11 different styles. You can use them for your own press releases. But first, let's consider writing headlines for some of the other promotional tools we've discussed.

Direct Mail, Flyers, and Brochures

The best headlines do three things: They identify the right target market, provide benefits, and generate enough interest to get the readers to read on. Let's look at each one in more depth.

- Identify the right target market: You need to make sure that members of your target market read your promotional publication. Your headline needs to speak immediately to them. There's nothing wrong with starting your headline with "MOTHERS" or even "ATTENTION Ladies 37–40 with no children." Of course, there are other more subtle ways, such as "Here's how to make your Ford go faster," or "Help your kids succeed at school this year."

- Provide Benefits: You need to give your readers reasons to investigate further. Think about it—what is really going to make them want to read on? A headline such as "MEN: How you can have twice as much sex as you're having now . . . guaranteed" speaks for itself. What can you say about your product or service—what is its main benefit? Once you've thought about that, try coming up with some more specific and interesting ways of phrasing it. For example, "How you can make an extra $4500 this year and pay off those credit card debts" is more interesting than "How you can make more money."

- Generate Interest: There's nothing more powerful than curiosity. Compare these two headlines: "AMWAY: A new future for you" and "How you make $1100 extra per week by meeting three new people each month." Both are for the same company, but one holds more interest value and is more likely to get you reading. Try getting the main benefit across without telling the whole story, and getting a bit of mystery in there at the same time. Of course, too much mystery can kill your whole campaign. Who'd read a publication with a headline such as "Pure Grunt," "Big Cheese," or "Stilted?" No one, as so many businesses have discovered.

Headline Starters

This is where you get to write potential headlines for your publication. You'll get a sharper focus of what you want to really say to editors, journalists, and recipients in general, as well as learning what makes a headline work.

Quotes

First, write two headlines that make use of what someone else has said about your product or service. Here are some examples:

> Leading authority claims George's Widgets are the best.

> George's Widgets are market leaders, says expert.

Now it's your turn.

Leading Authority _____

_____

Expert Claims _____

_____

Facts

Now, try two headlines using research figures or facts to back up your story. Here are some examples:

> Research shows that George's Widgets last longer.

> Studies prove George's Widgets are the best on the market.

Now it's your turn.

Research shows_____

_____

Studies prove _____

_____

write two headlines beginning with "Seven reasons" . . . Here are some Examples:

> Seven reasons why YOU should call George's Widgets today . . .

> Seven reasons to get your Widget from George's . . .

Now it's your turn.

Seven reasons _____

_____

Seven reasons _____

_____

Here's Why

Now, try two headlines beginning with "Here's why." Here are some examples:

> Here's why George is offering YOU a FREE box of Widgets.

> Here's why YOU need to call George's Widgets now.

Now it's your turn.

Here's why _____

_____

Here's why _____

_____

Here's How

Next, try two headlines beginning with "Here's how." Here are some good examples:

> Here's how George's Widgets can help you live forever.

> Here's how to get the perfect Widget . . . guaranteed.

Now it's your turn.

Here's how _____

_____

Here's how _____

_____

Announcing

Next, try two headlines beginning with "Announcing." Here are some examples:

Announcing . . . a Widget dealer that guarantees your delight.

Announcing . . . a guaranteed way to lose weight using Widgets.

Now it's your turn.

Announcing _____

_____

Announcing _____

_____

DON'T

Next, try two headlines beginning with "DON'T." Here are some great examples:

DON'T take another breath until you read this.

DON'T call anyone about Widgets until YOU speak to George.

Now it's your turn.

DON'T _____

_____

DON'T _____

_____

New

Next, try two headlines beginning with "New." Here are some examples:

New . . . widgets that actually repair themselves.

New, cheaper way to buy widgets.

Now it's your turn.

New _____

_____

New _____

_____

Now

Try two headlines beginning with "Now." Here are some examples:

Now available . . . home hairdressing kits your teenage daughter will like.

Now in preproduction . . . a movie based on the life of Elvis Presley.

Now it's your turn.

Now _____

_____

Now _____

_____

Company Name

Next, try two headlines beginning with your Company Name. Here are some examples:

George's Widget store to extend trading hours.

George's Widget store to employ 35 locals.

Now it's your turn.

Your company name_____

_____

Your company name_____

_____

Local

Finally, try two headlines beginning with "Local." Here are some examples:

Local manufacturer to export widgets.

Local Widget manufacturer wins top award.

Now it's your turn.

Local _____

_____

Local _____

_____

Part 7

▮ Creating Powerful Offers

So you've written a great headline, an exciting first paragraph, and subheadlines that tell a story. But what are you going to do to get your target market to respond? Great copy alone will not work; you need to have a strong offer, an offer that *you* would respond to.

So, What Is a Great Offer?

When thinking of what to offer your customers, ask yourself this: "If I read this publication, would the offer be good enough to make me respond?" If the answer is *no,* then go back to the drawing board. Without a great offer, you cannot achieve great results.

Another thing to consider when coming up with your offer is the lifetime value of the people who respond to your letter. Making a smaller profit in the short term will generally work out better in the long run.

Here are some examples of powerful offers:

- **Free Haircut.** For a hairdressing salon looking to increase its database.

- **Two Steak Dinners and Two Glasses of Wine for $10.** For a restaurant recruiting members for its VIP Club.

- **One New Release Video and a Large Pizza for $3.** For a video store promotion to recruit new members.

All of these offers have a "too-good-to-be-true" ring about them and are sure to get a great response. Weak offers will cause your promotional campaign to fail. Understand that your offer is the part of your letter that gets your customers to act now, and to buy from you rather than from your opposition.

Here are some examples of weak offers:

- **10 Percent Off.** This is not a big enough discount to generate interest. Of course, it will depend on the size of the purchase.

- **Call Now for Your Free Color Brochure.** So what? Everyone hands out brochures. Unless the product is something incredible, people won't respond.

- **Buy 9 and Get the 10th for 1/2 Price.** No one would respond to this offer. It's too small.

Types of Offers

Here are some offers that would be worth considering:

The Added Value with Soft Dollar Cost

Soft dollar cost refers to products, services, or added extras you can combine with your standard product to make it more attractive and increase its perceived value, but without adding much, if anything, to your costs.

For this strategy to be effective, the added extra must have a high-perceived value, in other words your customers must see the added benefit as being of great value.

The Package Offer

By packaging products and services together, you create a more marketable combination. There is a higher perceived value when products or services are packaged. Your customers will want to buy more, simply because of the extra products that they get when buying a product they already want.

One of the best examples of a great package is computer equipment. Buy the hardware and receive the software for free. This style of offer is very attractive to potential customers.

Discounts versus Bonus Offers

More often than not discounting will cost you profits. A far better way of clearing stock and generating extra trade is to have a "Two for the Price of One" sale. Or, try a "Buy one and Get one FREE" promotion.

The other way of putting this is "Every 10th purchase free," or "When you spend $100, we'll give you $20 off your next purchase."

Valued-at Offer

If you are including free items in your campaign, make sure you value them. For example, "CALL now for your FREE consultation, normally valued at $75." This positions your time, product, or service much more than a simple giveaway that people won't value or appreciate.

Time-Limited Offers

Place a time limit on your offer; it will dramatically increase the response rate because it gives people a reason to respond right now. Place urgency in your offer: "For a short time only," "Call before such and such," "Only while stocks last." These will all create a sense of urgency in your consumer's mind.

Guaranteed Offers

Using a guaranteed offer is a great way to boost the response to your promotional campaign. People will be far more willing to part with their money if you take the risk out of the buying decision. The better the guarantee you make, the higher your response rate will be.

Free Offers

Giving away something absolutely free (no catches whatsoever) is often a brilliant way to build a loyal customer base. Offer a "bribe" to get them in through the door initially, then great service and products to encourage them to come back. This type of offer can reduce your cost per lead dramatically.

Break-Even Analysis

It's essential you work out your costs up front. Otherwise, you'll have no idea what you need to achieve in order for the campaign to be worthwhile. You may find out after doing the analysis that the campaign has so little chance of success, you need to go back to the drawing board.

Bradley J. Sugars

This analysis is for the whole campaign. After you've worked out your total fixed costs (for the campaign), you then work out your profit (your average dollar sale minus your variable costs), which gives you enough information to work out how many responses you need in order to break even.

Divide this number by the total number of publications you are planning to send out. This will give you a percentage response rate. As a very rough guide (every case is different), anything over 15 percent is stretching it. If you need a higher response rate, you might want to rethink it.

For example, the very best campaigns aimed at cold, new lists get around a 15 percent response rate. In direct mail, for instance, the best campaigns to existing clients achieve around 60 percent. These are rare results—if you need higher than that to break even, reassess whether direct mail is the best way to go.

Break-Even Analysis

Lead Generation Campaign

Hard Costs

Advertising	$_____
Envelopes	$_____
Paper	$_____
Printing	$_____
Postage	$_____
Other	$_____
1. Total Fixed Costs	$_____
2. Average $$$ Sale	$_____

Variable Costs

Telephone	$_____
Wages	$_____

Electricity	$_____
Rent	$_____
Brochures	$_____
Other Postage	$_____
Other	$_____
3. Total Variables	$_____
Delivery Costs	
Cost of Goods Sold	$_____
Taxes	$_____
Transportation	$_____
Packaging	$_____
Other	$_____
4. Total Delivery	$_____
5. Net Profit [2/(3 + 4)]	$_____

Testing and Measuring

It's crucial that you understand the principle of testing and measuring. Just the same way you'd try different ads in the paper to see which one works the best, or different front counter displays to discover which one sold the most, you need to be prepared to change your promotional tools to find out which approach works the best.

Remember, it's always better to hand out 20 brochures that don't work, than 20,000. Even if you love your new brochure, and everyone who sees it goes crazy, it's important to keep your head and avoid going too far too soon.

The principles are the same no matter what promotional tool you're testing and measuring. But for the sake of clarity, I'll discuss the process you'll go through for a brochure.

Take it slowly at first. Check the response, and then gradually increase the numbers. If you hand out 100 brochures, and find that 10 of the coupons or ads from them come back, it should follow that 10,000 newsletters should turn into 1000 new sales. Of course, nothing is ever that certain in marketing or business, and you really have to wait and see.

Having said that, it's important to realize if you hand out 100 brochures and see none back, you'd be slightly insane to expect 10,000 to do much better.

You have the option of creating a number of versions of your brochure, and trying all versions at the same time. Ask people where they heard about you, and which brochure they have. Over time, you may notice one version seems to do much better than the others. This is the one you keep.

The problem is, creating newsletters can be expensive—there are the setup costs, then the printing costs. If you were to create multiple versions, you'd end up spending quite a deal more than if you just decided on one and stuck to it.

Ultimately, it depends on how important brochures are to your business. If they represent one of your most crucial sources of new business and repeat sales, then it may be in your best long-term interests to pay for two different brochures.

The other option is to create a small number (about 20) of each version you're thinking about using. Show these to as many people as you can—customers, friends, family. When they give you feedback, *listen* to what they have to say. Don't block out their criticism of your favorite design, or minimize their praise of the one you didn't like.

It pays to not be picky about it—this isn't fine art we're talking about. Your brochure is a business tool that is designed to make you money. Take note of what people say, and act accordingly.

When creating different versions, you should alter only the most important parts of the brochure. Changing the size of your phone number from 12 points to 16 points is unlikely to make much difference, but a new headline, a different offer, and a change in the amount of text will make a big difference.

If you're going to test two versions against each other, make sure they are significantly different. There's no point spending all that money only to put out two brochures that look virtually the same, save a couple of truly unimportant differences.

You'll find that changing the headline on the front panel, and the subheadlines in the main content, will completely change the amount of response you receive. Just as your brochure is an advertisement for your business, the headlines are the ads for the brochure's text.

Compare these two headlines:

"How to make more money"

and

"How 37,600 Australian women under 27 are making $2300 per week, every week without fail"

Which one would you read? The second headline definitely stimulates a hell of a lot more curiosity. Having said that, you can never be entirely sure which one will work the best. This is why testing and measuring is so important.

If you can understand that two headlines would bring in such a different response, you can understand why it's worth printing up a couple of versions and seeing which one takes off for you.

It's also important you really take proper note of which one is working the best. Create a tally sheet and make sure you fill it in every time somebody comes in in response to a brochure. After a month or so, add up the tally and see which one is working the best.

Worth Considering

There is a whole raft of other promotional tools worth considering. I'll touch on them briefly here, but if you need more information or assistance, contact your local *Action International* Business Coach.

Inserts

This is when you have your brochure or flyer inserted into a magazine or newspaper. The key here is having a strong offer. For example, a hairdressing salon offering free haircuts could expect a good result. Try using a picture that grabs attention and tells a story. A photograph of someone using your product is a good start. You might also consider printing the insert in such a way that it looks like part of the magazine or newspaper. This is sure to arouse the reader's curiosity.

Sidewalk Handbills

This type of promotion will generally work only for inexpensive, impulse-type products. Make sure you have a good offer before you start. You should then get a reasonable return.

Catalogs

Your catalogs need to be professionally printed. Remember, you need to list all the benefits of your products, not the features. People aren't interested in the fact that your new washing machine is made from stainless steel; they want to know that it will last and do the job, hassle free. Catalogs are normally better suited to retail stores rather than service-based companies. Make sure to include photographs of your products and that the benefits of each appear alongside the photograph.

White Pages

Every business needs to be listed in the White Pages. Although you're not going to get hundreds of calls from it, you will still get enough to warrant the phone call it takes to have your company listed.

Piggyback Invoice Mailings

This is where you get to include your flyer or brochure with the regular invoice mailings of another company. Even though your letter is certain to make it into the home and get looked at by people who may be in the market for your product or service, you need to give them a reason to call now. Include a powerful offer with your letter, and place a time limit on it to give it a sense of urgency.

Faxes

Don't fall into the trap of simply sending the same companies faxes on an ongoing basis. People will soon tire of this and begin to see it as an intrusion. If you've sent two faxes to the same company without a response, you'll need to find a different way to reach it. Be careful not to send faxes that are too long. It ties up the fax machine, preventing the company from receiving other faxes.

Sponsorships

You should ensure that the club you're sponsoring only deals with you and not your competition. Ensure that the members also come to you by building up an excellent rapport with them. It's also important that your logo appears on their apparel so that it can be clearly seen in photographs that may appear in the local newspapers. Companies such as butcher shops usually do well through this form of promotion, particularly if the club buys a number of meat trays or BBQ packs through them.

Postcard Mailings

You may also like to send prospective customers a postcard featuring an exotic location. You would then write on the back, explaining that they could be spending time in that very place if they take the action you want them to take. Give them the benefits of your offer without too much information about the offer itself. Try to get them excited and looking forward to hearing from you.

Internet Web Pages

The Internet has fast replaced mail-order catalogs in the United States, with many companies realizing the benefits of being able to sell anywhere in the world from the comfort of their own home. The Internet is a great medium for complex products, big-decision products, software, music, books, travel, and other related products. A common mistake made by many companies is making their Web sites too cluttered and difficult to read. Think of your site as if it were a print ad. Use a powerful headline and a strong offer to get people to call. Make sure they can place orders online using their credit cards.

Window Displays

Placing signs in your window displays, which list the benefit of your products, can be a great way to get your message across without scaring customers away. Make sure you paint a clear picture in the mind of the prospect about how much better life would be if they bought your product. This is also a good place to mention any guarantees or offers you have.

Bright colors and unusual themes attract attention. The more people you have looking at your window, the greater the chance they will venture inside. Also consider a joint promotion with another company for added impact.

Shopping Center Promotions

By setting up a display in a shopping center, you get the opportunity to demonstrate your goods or services to passing traffic. The trick here is to make it as interesting as possible. You'll need to have support material such as flyers, brochures, and business cards on hand to give out. Have someone with a microphone there to explain what you're doing and what the benefits are. By making your promotion interactive you can arouse great interest in your products. The more people who stand around looking, the more people who will be attracted to your display.

Conclusion

So there you have it—everything you need to get your business on the fast track to success.

Promotional strategies serve a very important purpose in business—any business. First they focus your mind and attention on what needs to be done to maximize your chances of achieving your business goals by generating more leads. Second, by developing them you could learn things about your business you never knew before.

Once you've worked your way through this book, you'll know how to write effective press releases. You'll know what it takes to produce brochures and flyers that work. You'll also know how to develop and implement an effective direct mail campaign.

And once you've seen what simple, yet effective, promotional strategies can do for your business, you'll be eager to try other promotional tools like those mentioned briefly in Part 6. These you'll be able to implement yourself because you'll have gained valuable "insider" knowledge on how to write killer headlines and create powerful offers that really work.

You'll also know how to analyze the costs involved and how to work out what your break-even point is. You'll quickly develop promotional campaigns that will be the envy of your competitors because you'll really understand how to test and measure every step of the way.

So, what are you waiting for? Get into *Action* now.

■ Getting into *Action*

So, when is the best time to start?

Now—right now—so let me give you a step-by-step method to get yourself onto the same success path of many of my clients and the clients of my team at *Action International.*

Start testing and measuring now.

You'll want to ask your customers and prospects how they found out about you and your business. This will give you an idea of what's been working and what hasn't. You also want to concentrate on the five areas of the business chassis. Remember:

1. Number of Leads from each campaign.
2. Conversion Rate from each and every campaign.
3. Number of Transactions on average per year per customer.
4. Average Dollar Sale from each campaign.
5. Your Margins on each product or service.

The Number of Leads is easy; just take a measure for four weeks, average it out, and multiply by 50 working weeks of the year. Of course you'd ask each lead where they came from so you've got enough information to make advertising decisions.

The Conversion Rate is a little trickier, not because it's hard to measure, but because we want to know a few more details. You want to know what level of conversion you have from each and every type of marketing strategy you use. Remember that some customers won't buy right away, so keep accurate records on each and every lead.

To find the Number of Transactions you'll need to go through your records. Hopefully you can find the transaction history of at least 50 of your past customers and then average out their yearly purchases.

The Average Dollar Sale is as simple as it sounds. The total dollars sold divided by the number of sales. The best information you can collect is the average from each marketing campaign you run, so that you know where the real profit is coming from.

And, of course, your margins. An Average Margin is good to know and measure, but to know the margins on everything you sell is the most powerful knowledge you can collect.

If you're having any challenges with your testing and measuring, be sure to contact your nearest *Action International* Business Coach. She'll be able to help you through and show you the specialized documents to use.

If, by chance, you're thinking of racing ahead before you test and measure, remember this. It's impossible to improve a score when you don't know what the score is.

So you've got your starting point. You know exactly what's going on in your business right now. In fact, you know more about not only what's happening right now, but also the factors that are going to create what will happen tomorrow.

The next step in your business growth is simple.

Let's decide what you want out of the business—in other words, your goals. Here are the main points I want you to plan for.

How many hours do you want to work each week? How much money do you want to take out of the business each month? And, most importantly, when do you want to finish the business?

By "finish" the business, I mean when it will be systematized enough so it can run without your having to be there. Remember this about business; a little bit of planning goes a long way, but to make a plan you have to have a destination.

Once again, if you're having difficulty, talk to an *Action International* Business Coach. He'll know exactly how to help you find what it is you really want out of both your business and your life.

Now the real work begins.

Remember, our goal is to get a 10 percent increase in each area over the next 12 months. Choose well, but I want to warn you of one thing, one thing I can literally guarantee.

Eight out of 10 marketing campaigns you run *will not work.*

That's why when you choose to run, say, an advertising campaign in your local newspaper, you've got to run at least 10 different ads. When you select a direct mail campaign, you should send out at least 10 different letters to test, and so on.

Make sure you get at least five strategies under each heading and plan to run at least one, preferably two, at least each month for the next 12 months.

Don't work on just one of the five areas at a time; mix it up a little so you get the synergy of all five areas working together.

Now, this is the most important advice I can give you:

Learn how to make each and every strategy work. Don't just think you know what to do; go through my hints and tips, read more books, listen to as many tapes as you can, watch all the videos you can find, talk to the experts, and make sure you get the most advantage you can before you invest a whole lot of money.

The next 12 months are going to be a matter of doing the numbers, running the campaigns, testing headlines, testing offers, testing prices, and, of course, measuring the results.

By the end of it you should have at least five new strategies in each of the five areas working together to produce a great result.

Once again I want to stress that this will work and this will make your business grow as long as *you* work it.

Is it simple? *Yes.*

Is it easy? *No.*

You'll have to work hard. If you can get the guidance of someone who's been there before you, then get it.

Whatever you do, start it now, start it today, and most importantly, make the most of every day. Your past does not equal your future; you decide your future right here and right now.

_Be_ who you want to be, _do_ what you need to do, in order to _have_ what you want to have.

Positive _thought_ without positive _Action_ leaves you with positively _nothing_. I called my company _Action International_, not Theory International, or Yeah, I read that book International, but _Action International_.

So take the first step—and get into _Action_.

■ ABOUT THE AUTHOR

Bradley J. Sugars

Brad Sugars is a world-renowned Australian entrepreneur, author, and business coach who has helped more than a million clients around the world find business and personal success.

He's a trained accountant, but as he puts it, most of his experience comes from owning his own companies. Brad's been in business for himself since age 15 in some way or another, although his father would argue he started at 7 when he was caught selling his Christmas presents to his brothers. He's owned and operated more than two dozen companies, from pizza to ladies fashion, from real estate to insurance and many more.

His main company, *Action International*, started from humble beginnings in the back bedroom of a suburban home in 1993 when Brad started teaching business owners how to grow their sales and marketing results. Now *Action* has nearly 1000 franchises in 19 countries and is ranked in the top 100 franchises in the world.

Brad Sugars has spoken on stage with the likes of Tom Hopkins, Brian Tracy, John Maxwell, Robert Kiyosaki, and Allen Pease, written books with people like Anthony Robbins, Jim Rohn, and Mark Victor Hansen, appeared on countless TV and radio programs and in literally hundreds of print articles around the globe. He's been voted as one of the Most Admired Entrepreneurs by the readers of *E-Spy* magazine—next to the likes of Rupert Murdoch, Henry Ford, Richard Branson, and Anita Roddick.

Today, *Action International* has coaches across the globe and is ranked as one of the Top 25 Fastest Growing Franchises on the planet as well as the #1 Business Consulting Franchise. The success of *Action International* is simply attributed to the fact that they apply the strategies their coaches use with business owners.

Brad is a proud father and husband, the chairman of a major childrens' charity and in his own words, "a very average golfer."

Check out Brad's Web site www.bradsugars.com and read the literally hundreds of testimonials from those who've gone before you.

■ RECOMMENDED READING LIST

ACTION INTERNATIONAL BOOK LIST

"The only difference between *you* now and *you* in 5 years' time will be the people you meet and the books you read." Charlie Tremendous Jones

"And, the only difference between *your* income now and *your* income in 5 years' time will be the people you meet, the books you read, the tapes you listen to, and then how *you* apply it all." Brad Sugars

- *The E-Myth Revisited* by Michael E. Gerber
- *My Life in Advertising & Scientific Advertising* by Claude Hopkins
- *Tested Advertising Methods* by John Caples
- *Building the Happiness Centered Business* by Dr. Paddi Lund
- *Write Language* by Paul Dunn & Alan Pease
- *7 Habits of Highly Effective People* by Steven Covey
- *First Things First* by Steven Covey
- *Awaken the Giant Within* by Anthony Robbins
- *Unlimited Power* by Anthony Robbins
- *22 Immutable Laws of Marketing* by Al Ries & Jack Trout
- *21 Ways to Build a Referral Based Business* by Brad Sugars
- *21 Ways to Increase Your Advertising Response* by Mark Tier
- *The One Minute Salesperson* by Spencer Johnson & Larry Wilson
- *The One Minute Manager* by Spencer Johnson & Kenneth Blanchard
- *The Great Sales Book* by Jack Collis
- *Way of the Peaceful Warrior* by Dan Millman
- *How to Build a Championship Team*—Six Audio tapes by Blair Singer
- Brad Sugars "Introduction to Sales & Marketing" 3-hour Video
- Leverage—Board Game by Brad Sugars
- *17 Ways to Increase Your Business Profits* booklet & tape by Brad Sugars. FREE OF CHARGE to Business Owners

*To order Brad Sugars' products from the recommended reading list, call your nearest *Action International* office today.

▮ The 18 Most Asked Questions about Working with an *Action International* Business Coach

And 18 great reasons why you'll jump at the chance to get your business flying and make your dreams come true

1. So who is *Action International?*

Action International is a business Coaching and Consulting company started in 1993 by entrepreneur and author Brad Sugars. With offices around the globe and business coaches from Singapore to Sydney to San Francisco, *Action International* has been set up with you, the business owner, in mind.

Unlike traditional consulting firms, *Action* is designed to give you both short-term assistance and long-term training through its affordable Mentoring approach. After 12 years teaching business owners how to succeed, *Action's* more than 10,000 clients and 1,000,000 seminar attendees will attest to the power of the programs.

Based on the sales, marketing, and business management systems created by Brad Sugars, your *Action* Coach is trained to not only show you how to increase your business revenues and profits, but also how to develop the business so that you as the owner work less and relax more.

Action International is a franchised company, so your local *Action* Coach is a fellow business owner who's invested her own time, money, and energy to make her business succeed. At *Action,* your success truly does determine our success.

2. And, why do I need a Business Coach?

Every great sports star, business person, and superstar is surrounded by coaches and advisors.

And, as the world of business moves faster and gets more competitive, it's difficult to keep up with both the changes in your industry and the innovations in sales, marketing, and management strategies. Having a business coach is no longer a luxury; it's become a necessity.

On top of all that, it's impossible to get an objective answer from yourself. Don't get me wrong. You can survive in business without the help of a Coach, but it's almost impossible to thrive.

A Coach *can* see the forest for the trees. A Coach will make you focus on the game. A Coach will make you run more laps than you feel like. A Coach will tell it like it is. A Coach will give you small pointers. A Coach will listen. A Coach will be your marketing manager, your sales director, your training coordinator, your partner, your confidant, your mentor, your best friend, and an *Action* Business Coach will help you make your dreams come true.

3. Then, what's an Alignment Consultation?

Great question. It's where an *Action* Coach starts with every business owner. You'll invest a minimum of $1295, and during the initial 2 to 3 hours your Coach invests with you, he'll learn as much as he can about your business, your goals, your challenges, your sales, your marketing, your finances, and so much more.

All with three goals in mind: To know exactly where your business is now. To clarify your goals both in the business and personally. And thirdly, to get the crucial pieces of information he needs to create your businesses *Action* Plan for the next 12 months.

Not a traditional business or marketing plan mind you, but a step-by-step plan of *Action* that you'll work through as you continue with the Mentor Program.

4. So, what, then, is the Mentor Program?

Simply put, it's where your *Action* Coach will work with you for a full 12 months to make your goals a reality. From weekly coaching calls and goal-setting sessions, to creating marketing pieces together, you will develop new sales strategies and business systems so you can work less and learn all that you need to know about how to make your dreams come true.

You'll invest between $995 and $10,000 a month and your Coach will dedicate a minimum of 5 hours a month to working with you on your sales, marketing, team building, business development, and every step of the *Action* Plan you created from your Alignment Consultation.

Unlike most consultants, your *Action* Coach will do more than just show you what to do. She'll be with you when you need her most, as each idea takes shape, as each campaign is put into place, as you need the little pointers on making it happen, when you need someone to talk to, when you're faced with challenges and, most importantly, when you're just not sure what to do next. Your Coach will be there every step of the way.

5. Why at least 12 months?

If you've been in business for more than a few weeks, you've seen at least one or two so called "quick fixes."

Most Consultants seem to think they can solve all your problems in a few hours or a few days. At *Action* we believe that long-term success means not just scraping the surface and doing it for you. It means doing it with you, showing you how to do it, working alongside you, and creating the success together.

Over the 12 months, you'll work on different areas of your business, and month by month you'll not only see your goals become a reality, you'll gain both the confidence and the knowledge to make it happen again and again, even when your first 12 months of Coaching is over.

6. How can you be sure this will work in my industry and in my business?

Very simple. You see at *Action,* we're experts in the areas of sales, marketing, business development, business management, and team building just to name a few. With 328 different profit-building strategies, you'll soon see just how powerful these systems are.

You, on the other hand, are the expert in your business and together we can apply the *Action* systems to make your business fly.

Add to this the fact that within the *Action* Team at least one of our Coaches has either worked with, managed, worked in, or even owned a business that's the same or very similar to yours. Your *Action* Coach has the full resources of the entire *Action* team to call upon for every challenge you have. Imagine hundreds of experts ready to help you.

7. Won't this just mean more work?

Of course when you set the plan with your *Action* Coach, it'll all seem like a massive amount of work, but no one ever said attaining your goals would be easy.

In the first few months, it'll take some work to adjust, some work to get over the hump so to speak. The further you are into the program, the less and less work you'll have to do.

You will, however, be literally amazed at how focused you'll be and how much you'll get done. With focus, an *Action* Coach, and most importantly the *Action* Systems, you'll be achieving a whole lot more with the same or even less work.

8. How will I find the time?

Once again the first few months will be the toughest, not because of an extra amount of work, but because of the different work. In fact, your *Action* Coach will show you how to, on a day-to-day basis, get more work done with less effort.

In other words, after the first few months you'll find that you're not working more, just working differently. Then, depending on your goals from about month six onwards, you'll start to see the results of all your work, and if you choose to, you can start working less than ever before. Just remember, it's about changing what you do with your time, *not* putting in more time.

9. How much will I need to invest?

Nothing, if you look at it from the same perspective as we do. That's the difference between a cost and an investment. Everything you do with your *Action* Coach is a true investment in your future.

Not only will you create great results in your business, but you'll end up with both an entrepreneurial education second to none, and the knowledge that you can repeat your successes over and over again.

As mentioned, you'll need to invest at least $1295 up to $5000 for the Alignment Consultation and Training Day, and then between $995 and $10,000 a month for the next 12 months of coaching.

Your Coach may also suggest several books, tapes, and videos to assist in your training, and yes, they'll add to your investment as you go. Why? Because having an *Action* Coach is just like having a marketing manager, a sales team leader, a trainer, a recruitment specialist, and corporate consultant all for half the price of a secretary.

10. Will it cost me extra to implement the strategies?

Once again, give your *Action* Coach just half an hour and he'll show you how to turn your marketing into an investment that yields sales and profits rather than just running up your expenses.

In most cases we'll actually save you money when we find the areas that aren't working for you. But yes, I'm sure you'll need to spend some money to make some money.

Yet, when you follow our simple testing and measuring systems, you'll never risk more than a few dollars on each campaign, and when we find the ones that work, we make sure you keep profiting from them time and again.

Remember, when you go the accounting way of saving costs, you can only ever add a few percent to the bottom line.

Following Brad Sugars' formula, your *Action* Coach will show you that through sales, marketing, and income growth, your possible returns are exponential.

The sky's the limit, as they say.

11. Are there any guarantees?

To put it bluntly, no. Your *Action* Coach will never promise any specific results, nor will she guarantee that any of your goals will become a reality.

You see, we're your coach. You're still the player, and it's up to you to take the field. Your Coach will push you, cajole you, help you, be there for you, and even do some things with you, but you've still got to do the work.

Only *you* can ever be truly accountable for your own success and at *Action* we know this to be a fact. We guarantee to give you the best service we can, to answer your questions promptly, and with the best available information. And, last but not least your *Action* Coach is committed to making you successful whether you like it or not.

That's right, once we've set the goals and made the plan, we'll do whatever it takes to make sure you reach for that goal and strive with all your might to achieve all that you desire.

Of course we'll be sure to keep you as balanced in your life as we can. We'll make sure you never compromise either the long-term health and success of your company or yourself, and more importantly your personal set of values and what's important to you.

12. What results have other business owners seen?

Anything from previously working 60 hours a week down to working just 10—right through to increases in revenues of 100s and even 1000s of percent. Results speak for themselves. Be sure to keep reading for specific examples of real people, with real businesses, getting real results.

There are three reasons why this will work for you in your business. Firstly, your *Action* Coach will help you get 100 percent focused on your goals and the step-by-step processes to get you there. This focus alone is amazing in its effect on you and your business results.

Secondly, your coach will hold you accountable to get things done, not just for the day-to-day running of the business, but for the dynamic growth of the business. You're investing in your success and we're going to get you there.

Thirdly, your Coach is going to teach you one-on-one as many of *Action's* 328 profit-building strategies as you need. So whether your goal is to be making more money, or working fewer hours or both inside the next 12 months your goals can become a reality. Just ask any of the thousands of existing *Action* clients, or more specifically, check out the results of 19 of our most recent clients shown later in this section.

13. What areas will you coach me in?

There are five main areas your *Action* Coach will work on with you. Of course, how much of each depends on you, your business, and your goals.

Sales. The backbone of creating a superprofitable business, and one area we'll help you get spectacular results in.

Marketing and Advertising. If you want to get a sale, you've got to get a prospect. Over the next 12 months your *Action* Coach will teach you Brad Sugars' amazingly simple streetwise marketing—marketing that makes profits.

Team Building and Recruitment. You'll never *wish* for the right people again. You'll have motivated and passionate team members when your Coach shows you how.

Systems and Business Development. Stop the business from running you and start running your business. Your Coach will show you the secrets to having the business work, even when you're not there.

Customer Service. How to deliver consistently, make it easy to buy, and leave your customers feeling delighted with your service. Both referrals and repeat business are centered in the strategies your Coach will teach you.

14. Can you also train my people?

Yes. We believe that training your people is almost as important as coaching you.

Your investment starts at $1500 for your entire team, and you can decide between five very powerful in-house training programs. From "*Sales Made Simple*" for your face-to-face sales team to "*Phone Power*" for your entire team's telephone etiquette and sales ability. Then you can run the *"Raving Fans"* customer service training or the *"Total Team"* training. And finally, if you're too busy earning a living to make any real money, then you've just got to attend our *"Business Academy 101."* It will make a huge impact on your finances, business, career, family, and lifestyle. You'll be amazed at how much involvement and excitement comes out of your team with each training program.

15. Can you write ads, letters, and marketing pieces for me?

Yes. Your *Action* Coach can do it for you, he can train you to do it yourself, or we can simply critique the marketing pieces you're using right now.

If you want us to do it for you, our one-time fees start at just $1195. You'll not only get one piece; we'll design several pieces for you to take to the market and see which one performs the best. Then, if it's a critique you're after, just $349 means we'll work through your entire piece and give you feedback on what to change, how to change it, and what else you should do. Last but not least, for between $15 and $795 we can recommend a variety of books, tapes, and most importantly, Brad Sugars' Instant Success series books that'll take you step-by-step through the how-tos of creating your marketing pieces.

16. Why do you also recommend books, tapes, and videos?

Basically, to save you time and money. Take Brad Sugars' *Sales Rich* DVD or Video Series, for instance. In about 16 hours you'll learn more about business than you have in the last 12 years. It'll also mean your *Action* Coach works with you on the high-level implementation rather than the very basic teaching.

It's a very powerful way for you to speed up the coaching process and get phenomenal rather than just great results.

17. When is the best time to get started?

Yesterday. OK, seriously, right now, today, this minute, before you take another step, waste another dollar, lose another sale, work too many more hours, miss another family event, forget another special occasion.

Far too many business people wait and see. They think working harder will make it all better. Remember, what you know got you to where you are. To get to where you want to go, you've got to make some changes and most probably learn something new.

There's no time like the present to get started on your dreams and goals.

18. So how do we get started?

Well, you'd better get back in touch with your *Action* Coach. There's some very simple paperwork to sign, and then you're on your way.

You'll have to invest a few hours showing them everything about your business. Together you'll get a plan created and then the work starts. Remember, it may seem like a big job at the start, but with a Coach, you're sharing the load and together you'll achieve great things.

Here's what others say about what happened after working with an *Action* business coach

Paul and Rosemary Rose—Icontact Multimedia

"Our *Action* coach showed us several ways to help market our product. We went on to triple our client base and simultaneously tripled our profits in just seven months. It was unbelievable! Last year was our best Christmas ever. We were really able to spoil ourselves!"

S. Ford—Pride Kitchens

"In 6 months, I've gone from working more than 60 hours per week in my business to less than 20, and my conversion rate's up from 19 percent to 62 percent. I've now got some life back!"

Gary and Leanne Paper—Galea Timber Products

"We achieved our goal for the 12 months within a 6-month period with a 100 percent increase in turnover and a good increase in margins. We have already recommended and will continue to recommend this program to others."

Russell, Kevin, John, and Karen—Northern Lights Power and Distribution

"Our profit margin has increased from 8 percent to 21 percent in the last 8 months. *Action* coaching focussed us on what are our most profitable markets."

Ty Pedersen—De Vries Marketing Sydney

"After just three months of coaching, my sales team's conversion rate has grown from an average of less than 12 percent to more than 23 percent and our profits have climbed by more than 30 percent."

Hank Meerkerk and Hemi McGarvey—B.O.P. School of Welding

"Last year we started off with a profit forecast, but as soon as we got *Action* involved we decided to double our forecast. We're already well over that forecast again by two-and-a-half times on turnover, and profits are even higher. Now we run a really profitable business."

Stuart Birch—Education Personnel Limited

"One direct mail letter added $40,000 to my bottom line, and working with *Action* has given me quality time to work on my business and spend time with my family."

Mark West—Wests Pumping and Irrigation

"In four months two simple strategies have increased our business more than 20 percent. We're so busy, we've had to delay expanding the business while we catch up!"

Michael Griffiths—Gym Owner

"I went from working 70 hours per week *in* the business to just 25 hours, with the rest of the time spent working *on* the business."

Cheryl Standring—In Harmony Landscapes

"We tried our own direct mail and only got a 1 percent response. With *Action* our response rate increased to 20 percent. It's definitely worth every dollar we've invested."

Jason and Chris Houston—Empradoor Finishing

"After 11 months of working with *Action,* we have increased our sales by 497 percent, and the team is working without our having to be there."

Michael Avery—Coomera Pet Motels

"I was skeptical at first, but I knew we needed major changes in our business. In 2 months, our extra profits were easily covering our investment and our predictions for the next 10 months are amazing."

Garry Norris—North Tax & Accounting

"As an accountant, my training enables me to help other business people make more money. It is therefore refreshing when someone else can help me do the same. I have a policy of only referring my clients to people who are professional, good at what they do, and who have personally given me great service. *Action* fits all three of these criteria, and I recommend *Action* to my business clients who want to grow and develop their businesses further."

Bradley J. Sugars

Lisa Davis and Steve Groves—Mt. Eden Motorcycles

"With *Action* we increased our database from 800 to 1200 in 3 months. We consistently get about 20 new qualified people on our database each week for less than $10 per week."

Christine Pryor—U-Name-It Embroidery

"Sales for August this year have increased 352 percent. We're now targeting a different market and we're a lot more confident about what we're doing."

Joseph Saitta and Michelle Fisher—Banyule Electrics

"Working with *Action,* our inquiry rate has doubled. In four months our business has changed so much our customers love us. It's a better place for people to work and our margins are widening."

Kevin and Alison Snook—Property Sales

"In the 12 months previous to working with *Action,* we had sold one home in our subdivision. In the first eight months of working with *Action,* we sold six homes. The results speak for themselves."

Wayne Manson—Hospital Supplies

"When I first looked at the Mentoring Program it looked expensive, but from the inside looking out, its been the best money I have ever spent. Sales are up more than $3000 per month since I started, and the things I have learned and expect to learn will ensure that I will enjoy strong sustainable growth in the future."

▌*Action* Contact Details

***Action International* Asia Pacific**

Ground Floor, *Action* House, 2 Mayneview Street, Milton QLD 4064

Ph: +61 (0) 7 3368 2525

Fax: +61 (0) 7 3368 2535

Free Call: 1800 670 335

***Action International* Europe**

Olympic House, Harbor Road, Howth, Co. Dublin, Ireland

Ph: +353 (0) 1-8320213

Fax: +353 (0) 1-8394934

***Action International* North America**

5670 Wynn Road Suite A & C, Las Vegas, Nevada 89118

Ph: +1 (702) 795 3188

Fax: +1 (702) 795 3183

Free Call: (888) 483 2828

***Action International* UK**

3-5 Richmond Hill, Richmond, Surrey, TW 106RE

Ph: +44 020 8948 5151

Fax: +44 020 8948 4111

Action Offices around the globe:

Australia | Canada | China | England | France | Germany | Hong Kong

India | Indonesia | Ireland | Malaysia | Mexico | New Zealand

Phillippines | Scotland | Spain | Singapore | USA | Wales

Here's how you can profit from all of Brad's ideas with your local *Action* International **Business Coach**

Just like a sporting coach pushes an athlete to achieve optimum performance, provides them with support when they are exhausted, and teaches the athlete to execute plays that the competition does not anticipate.

A business coach will make you run more laps than you feel like. A business coach will show it like it is. And a business coach will listen.

The role of an *Action* Business Coach is to show you how to improve your business through guidance, support, and encouragement. Your coach will help you with your sales, marketing, management, team building, and so much more. Just like a sporting coach, your *Action* Business Coach will help you and your business perform at levels you never thought possible.

Whether you've been in business for a week or 20 years, it's the right time to meet with and see how you'll profit from an *Action* Coach.

As the owner of a business it's hard enough to keep pace with all the changes and innovations going on in your industry, let alone to find the time to devote to sales, marketing, systems, planning and team management, and then to run your business as well.

As the world of business moves faster and becomes more competitive, having a Business Coach is no longer a luxury; it has become a necessity. Based on the sales, marketing, and business management systems created by Brad Sugars, your *Action* Coach is trained to not only show you how to increase your business revenues and profits but also how to develop your business so that you, as the owner, can take back control. All with the aim of your working less and relaxing more. Making money is one thing; having the time to enjoy it is another.

Your *Action* Business Coach will become your marketing manager, your sales director, your training coordinator, your confidant, your mentor. In short, your *Action* Coach will help you make your business dreams come true.

ATTENTION BUSINESS OWNERS
You can increase your profits now

Here's how you can have one of Brad's *Action* *International* Business Coaches guide you to success.

Like every successful sporting icon or team, a business needs a coach to help it achieve its full potential. In order to guarantee your business success, you can have one of Brad's team as your business coach. You will learn about how you can get amazing results with the help of the team at **Action** *International*.

The business coaches are ready to take you and your business on a journey that will reward you for the rest of your life. You see, we believe **Action** speaks louder than words.

Complete and post this card to your local **Action** office to discover how our team can help you increase your income today!

Action *International*

The World's Number-1 Business Coaching Team

Name ....

Position ....

Company ....

Address ....

....

Country ....

Phone ....

Fax ....

Email ....

Referred by ....

How do I become an *Action* International **Business Coach?**

If you choose to invest your time and money in a great business and you're looking for a white-collar franchise opportunity to build yourself a lifestyle, an income, a way to take control of your life and, a way to get great personal satisfaction …

Then you've just found the world's best team!

Now, it's about finding out if you've got what it takes to really enjoy and thrive in this amazing business opportunity.

Here are the 4 things we look for in every *Action* Coach:

1. You've got to love succeeding

We're looking for people who love success, who love getting out there and making things happen. People who enjoy mixing with other people, people who thrive on learning and growing, and people who want to charge an hourly rate most professionals only dream of.

2. You've got to love being in charge of your own life

When you're ready to take control, the key is to be in business for yourself, but not by yourself. **Action**'s support, our training, our world leading systems, and the backup of a global team are all waiting to give you the best chance of being an amazing business success.

3. You've got to love helping people

Being a great Coach is all about helping yourself by helping others. The first time clients thank you for showing them step by step how to make more money and work less within their business, will be the day you realize just how great being an **Action** Business Coach really is.

4. You've got to love a great lifestyle

Working from home, setting your own timetable, spending time with family and friends, knowing that the hard work you do is for your own company and, not having to climb a so-called corporate ladder. This is what lifestyle is all about. Remember, business is supposed to give you a life, not take it away.

Our business is booming and we're seriously looking for people ready to find out more about how becoming a member of the **Action** *International* Business Coaching team is going to be the best decision you've ever made.

Apply online now at www.action-international.com

Here's how you can network, get new leads, build yourself an instant sales team, learn, grow and build a great team of supportive business owners around you by checking into your local *Action* Profit Club

Joining your local *Action* Profit Club is about more than just networking, it's also the learning and exchanging of profitable ideas.

Embark on a journey to a more profitable enterprise by meeting with fellow, like-minded business owners.

An **Action** Profit Club is an excellent way to network with business people and business owners. You will meet every two weeks for breakfast to network and learn profitable strategies to grow your business.

Here are three reasons why **Action** *International's* Profit Clubs work where other networking groups don't:

1. You know networking is a great idea. The challenge is finding the time and maintaining the motivation to keep it up and make it a part of your business. If you're not really having fun and getting the benefits, you'll find it gets easier to find excuses that stop you going. So, we guarantee you will always have fun and learn a lot from your bi-weekly group meetings.
2. The real problem is that so few people do any work 'on' their business. Instead they generally work "in" it, until it's too late. By being a member of an **Action** Profit Club, you get to attend FREE business-building workshops run by Business Coaches that teach you how to work "on" your business and avoid this common pitfall and help you to grow your business.
3. Unlike other groups, we have marketing systems to assist in your groups' growth rather than just relying on you to bring in new members. This way you can concentrate on YOUR business rather than on ours.

Latest statistics show that the average person knows at least 200 other contacts. By being a member of your local **Action** Profit Club, you have an instant network of around 3,000 people

Join your local *Action* Profit Club today.

Apply online now at www.actionprofitclub.com

LEVERAGE—The Game of Business
Your Business Success is just a Few Games Away

Leverage—The Game of Business is a fun way to learn how to succeed in business fast.

The rewards start flowing the moment you start playing!

Leverage is three hours of fun, learning, and discovering how you can be an amazingly successful business person.

It's a breakthrough in education that will have you racking up the profits in no time. The principles you take away from playing this game will set you up for a life of business success. It will open your mind to what's truly possible. Apply what you learn and **sit back and watch your profits soar.**

By playing this fun and interactive business game, you will learn:

- How to quickly raise your business income
- How business people can become rich and successful in a short space of time
- How to create a business that works without you

Isn't it time you had the edge over your competition?

Leverage has been played by all age groups from 12-85 and has been a huge learning experience for all. The most common comment we hear is: 'I thought I knew a lot, and just by playing a simple board game I have realized I have a long way to go. The knowledge I've gained from playing Leverage will make me thousands! Thanks for the lesson.'

To order your copy online today, please visit www.bradsugars.com